PRAISE FO[illegible]

"Big idea alert! If you or your team have the need to identify and develop a big idea—buy and read this book! It is an empowering, enlightening, delightful read."

TIM TEMPLETON, best-selling author, *The Referral of a Lifetime*

"Powerful! Pure wisdom applied in a simple formula to get out of 'stuck.' My mind has been set free as I have applied the simple principles of *Big Ideas*!"

JEFF STUTZ, Marketing strategist from start-ups to billion dollar brands, speaker and entrepreneur

"Having read the book and experienced the Big Ideas workshop, I can personally vouch for how the principles drive innovative thinking and creativity. This is a must read for anyone who wants to have bigger and better ideas!"

RYAN LAWS, CEO, *Pro Image Sports*

"*Big Ideas* is a must-read if you want to think on a higher level and have your ideas translate into executable solutions."

SPENCER REESE, Partner, *Reese Poyfair Richards, PLLC*

"The idea that there is a proven way to have more aha moments is energizing and fun. Big ideas are just around the corner!"

MICHAEL BRESHEARS, CEO, *Kyani*

"This is a great book for anyone looking for better answers. *Big Ideas* drives home the message that anyone can be more creative. Everyone should read *Big Ideas*."

GARRETT MCGRATH, Entrepreneur, President, *Association of Network Marketing Professionals*

"I love books that illuminate better ways to think and *Big Ideas* is such a book. It's a book for anyone who wants to upgrade their thinking."

JD BREWER, CEO, *Metcom Studios*

"I wrote the book *Promptings* to act as a guide for paying attention and acting. The book *Big Ideas* is a perfect companion. This is a book for everyone."

KODY BATEMAN, Founder and CEO, *SendoutCards*, best-selling author of *Promptings* and *The Power of Human Connection*

BIG IDEAS

INSPIRED
SOLUTIONS
Publishing

FOREWORD BY STEPHEN M.R. COVEY

BIG IDEAS

HOW TO UNLEASH YOUR CREATIVE SELF AND HAVE MORE AHA! MOMENTS

CRAIG CASE

JENNIFER BECKSTRAND

ACKNOWLEDGEMENTS

In appreciation to Breck England who added much to the development of the ideas presented in this book.

BIG IDEAS: How to Unleash Your Creative Self and Have More Aha! Moments

Craig Case & Jennifer Beckstrand

Published by Inspired Solutions Publishing
Salt Lake City, Utah 84101
801-891-3277
inspiredsolutionspublishing.com

To order additional copies call 801-891-3277, go to *Amazon.com* or *inspiredsolutionspublishing.com*

Image credits: Stefan Malmesjö (Flickr), Hannes Wolf (Unsplash)

Book design by Morgan Crockett

ISBN 978-0-9976993-2-6 (Softcover)
ISBN 978-0-9976993-3-3 (eBook)
ISBN 978-0-9976993-4-0 (Audiobook)

Printed in the United States of America

To Marsha, who teaches me daily by her quiet and gentle example.
CRAIG

To Gary, my best friend. So glad we're on this journey together.
JENNIFER

CONTENTS

FOREWORD

Ideas.

Insights.

Solutions.

Do you need more of these in your life and work? This wonderful book, *Big Ideas*, will powerfully pave the way for you to find the answers to the questions you face.

When I was working on my first book, *The Speed of Trust*, the publisher told us we needed to shorten the book 25 percent. It was like cutting muscle–almost bone. We had already spent months crafting stories and documenting data that had taken years to compile. How could I cut 25 percent of my life's work to that point?

It had to be done.

Following a similar process as is outlined in this book, we made the cuts, and it produced an even better book. I was inspired at each step of the way and am grateful I listened to the editor's recommendation and my unconscious mind.

I first met Craig Case when we worked together at FranklinCovey many years ago. He is an original thinker who used innovative solutions to address his clients' distinctive needs. Craig's practical application of the principles showcased in this book, combined with his rigorous research, produced great results for those clients and our company. I met Jennifer Beckstrand while working on projects with her husband years ago at FranklinCovey. Jennifer is an extremely talented and creative writer and storyteller. The blending of their gifts makes for a very readable and engaging book that will help you find solutions to the opportunities that lie in front of you as well as to the problems you face.

Three aspects of this book stand out for me:

First, the brain science. Neuroscience is one of the great frontiers in science and medicine today. What scientists have learned about our brains in the last fifteen years dwarfs what was understood before that time. I find the data and studies cited in this book compelling. This work is not merely the opinion of the authors; it is sound science based on a number of worthwhile studies.

Second, the practical nature of the Big Ideas Model. While the authors cite examples of Nobel Prize winners, world-class poets, musicians, scientists, innovators, and business people, the Big Ideas Model is not for the privileged few. Everyone can follow and benefit from the step-by-step process Craig and Jennifer have so elegantly outlined.

Third, the abundant examples and stories. Reading brain science and following a process can seem lifeless—but not on the trip you'll take through fascinating stories and revelatory examples of how people have discovered the dividends of inspired ideas.

I highly recommend this insightful book to all readers who desire to find and apply lasting solutions to both small and challenging situations. *Big Ideas* will help you in all aspects of your life and work, and I'm hopeful you'll find it as valuable as I did.

–Stephen M. R. Covey

Author of *The New York Times* and #1 *Wall Street Journal* bestselling book, *The Speed of Trust*, and Co-founder of FranklinCovey's Trust Practice

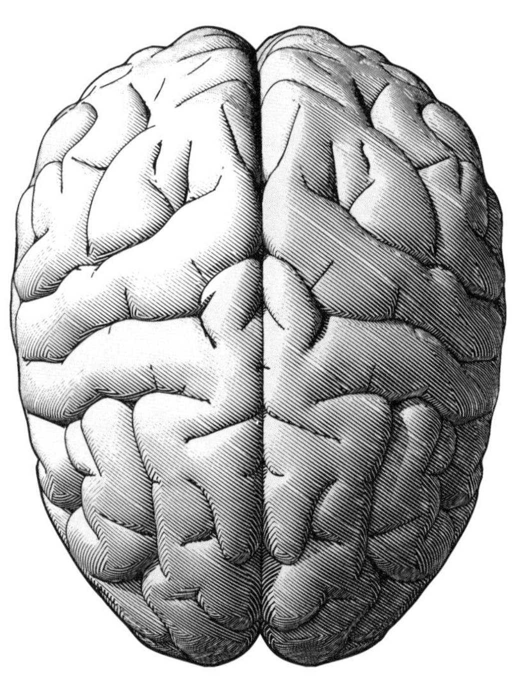

INTRODUCTION

YOU HAVE PROBLEMS—MIND-BENDING, FRUSTRATING, ANNOYING PROBLEMS. You need solutions. You need good ideas, and you need to know how to get them.

Where do you start in the search for ideas?

And not just good ideas, but profound, focused, life-changing ideas?

Big ideas.

Is it possible to boost your creativity? To discover far-reaching solutions to difficult problems? To develop innovative ideas that not only improve your life but catapult it in a better direction?

Yes, it is. And we're going to show you how.

Every great discovery, creation, or invention has its genesis in a problem. The search for solutions is how big ideas come about. And big ideas can change the world.

At the beginning of the fifteenth century, only thirty thousand books existed in all of Europe, roughly one book for every twelve hundred people on the continent. Books were assembled by hand, each book requiring approximately two years to produce. Such painstaking construction rendered each book prohibitively expensive. In today's currency, the average European made fifteen cents a day, and a book cost about two hundred dollars, roughly two to three years' income. Only the Church or the very wealthy could afford to own books.

To Johannes Gutenberg, the rarity of books was an enormous problem begging for a solution.

As a metallurgist and inventor, Gutenberg often had more ideas than he had money. Cash to fund his business and his ideas was always in short supply. Gutenberg also had a passion for reading and was troubled by the expense and rarity of books. Literacy was expanding from the clergy to the wider population, but what good was literacy when there was little to read?

These problems dominated Gutenberg's thoughts. Possible solutions captivated his imagination. For years, Gutenberg struggled for answers. How could he produce books faster and more inexpensively? Was it possible to open the floodgates of knowledge for the masses and not just the wealthy few?

Gutenberg was running short on funds and ready to give up when, in an instant, an answer came. In Gutenberg's own words, the solution manifested itself to his mind, "like a ray of light."[1] Printing with a press using movable type was his inspired, revolutionary idea.

It took Gutenberg ten years to raise the money, but once his printing press was operational, book production exploded. Within fifty years, there were over one thousand movable type printing presses in Europe and forty million books available on more than 14,000 subjects. Instead of two to three years of salary, a book could be purchased for a day's pay. By 1600, there were over two hundred million new books in existence.[2] Information and learning exploded, and in one generation the world was changed forever.

Gutenberg's press is arguably the most important invention in the history of the world.

What happened in Gutenberg's brain when he had his big idea, and can such creativity be replicated? Can the average person have big ideas like Gutenberg?

The world is becoming increasingly unpredictable and complex, and with this complexity comes the need for groundbreaking ways to navigate the maze. According to a recent IBM survey of more than 1,500 CEOs from sixty countries and thirty-three industries, top executives believe that creativity and innovation are of greater importance in addressing this complexity than are rigor, discipline, integrity, or even vision.[3]

It's not necessary to be a CEO to appreciate the need for better answers to life's endless challenges. We all have problems that beg for solutions. Whether we want to compose a symphony, feed a starving population, cure a disease, balance a budget, write a book, or heal a broken relationship, we all need more inspiration and big ideas.

Usually, our most pressing problems don't have simple answers. Solutions require thought, hard work, and inspiration. In this book, you'll learn how to harness the power of your mind to access creativity, innovation, and big ideas, like Johannes Gutenberg was able to do.

This book is for anyone trying to solve problems—creative, business, personal, or academic. It is a book for those who have puzzling difficulties but few answers.

For over a century, the intangible Aha! Moment has been the subject of extensive scientific study. Experiments to discover what happens in the brain during an Aha! Moment have led to fascinating discoveries about how our brains can generate more and better ideas.

The chapters ahead examine revolutionary ideas and the people who created them, current brain science theory and what happens in your head when you have a big idea, and thinking models that help generate Aha! Moments. In this book, you'll find out how anyone, including you, can have more big ideas.

Solutions start here.

PART ONE

THE NEED FOR BIG IDEAS

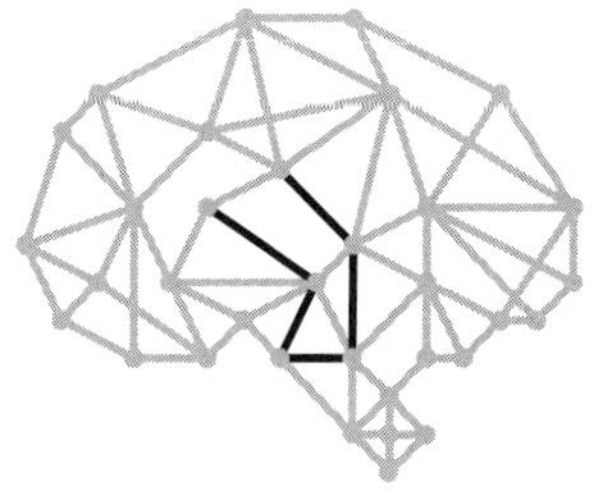

THE NATURE OF BIG IDEAS

"Imagination is the source of all human achievement."
–Sir Ken Robinson

IN THE THIRD CENTURY BC, King Hiero II of Syracuse commissioned a goldsmith to make him a splendid crown of pure gold, providing the goldsmith with two pounds of gold for the project. A few weeks later, the goldsmith delivered the king an exquisitely wrought crown weighing exactly two pounds. The king was pleased and paid the goldsmith handsomely.

Soon afterward, Hiero heard rumors that the goldsmith had cheated him by substituting cheaper metals in the crown for half a pound of the gold and keeping the rest of the gold for himself. The king was furious, but he had no way of knowing if he'd been tricked.

Archimedes, a well-known mathematician and inventor in Syracuse, was ordered to determine if the crown was pure gold without melting it down or damaging it in any way. Some versions of the story say that the king threatened Archimedes with his life if he failed.

For weeks, Archimedes labored with the problem, but he couldn't figure out a way to measure the crown's density without destroying it. Discouraged and frightened, Archimedes prepared for his daily bath, deciding to forget about the problem while he relaxed his aching body. As he lowered himself into the bath, the water rose. He continued to descend, and the water overflowed from the tub. In an instant, he realized he had found the solution to the crown problem. He was so excited by his sudden discovery, he ran naked through the city streets shouting, "Eureka! Eureka!" which means, "I have found it! I have found it!"

What Archimedes discovered was the principle of displacement. Like a person in a tub of water, the submerged crown would displace an amount of water equal to its own volume. In this way, Archimedes could determine the crown's density without melting it down. If the crown's density was lower than two pounds of pure gold, Archimedes would be able to prove that the goldsmith had used cheaper, less-dense metals in the crown.

Archimedes found that the crown did displace less water than a lump of gold of equal weight. He concluded the crown was not pure gold and the goldsmith had indeed used less-expensive metals in the king's crown. According to some sources, the goldsmith was executed for his deceit.

This sudden, brilliant moment of insight is not unique to Archimedes. What he experienced has been repeated again and again by scientists and inventors, artists and musicians, architects and soldiers, writers and poets.

A sudden illumination of the mind, like the kind Archimedes experienced in his bath, has been called many things. You may have heard of a flash of insight referred to as one of these:

An Aha! Moment

A Eureka Experience

An Epiphany

A Gamma Spike

An Inner Voice

Inspiration

In this book we refer to such experiences as Aha! Moments or Big Ideas. They are often paradigm shifting, life transforming, and even world changing. They all point to a remarkable mental phenomenon of enhanced awareness and understanding coupled with a kind of euphoria beyond our ability to create on our own.

Great scientists like Marie Curie and Albert Einstein had flashes of insight. Writers and artists like Leonardo Da Vinci, George R.R. Martin, and Maya Angelou experienced inspiration and epiphanies. Inventors like Thomas Edison and Mary Anderson had Aha! Moments, or Big Ideas.

In the 1930s, Albert Einstein's work was at a standstill. In an effort to overcome his mental block, he reached out to the poet Saint-John Perse,[4] hoping to learn something about how the writer's mind works. "How does a poet work? How does the idea of a poem come? How does this idea grow?"

Persei responded, describing how intuition, imagination, and the subconscious played into his creativity.

"But it is the same for a man of science!" Einstein replied. "The mechanics of discovery are neither logical or intellectual. It is a sudden illumination, almost a rapture. Later, to be sure, intelligence analyzes and experiments confirm (or invalidate) the intuition. But initially there is a great forward leap of the imagination."[5]

The word *inspiration* literally means "in-spirit," an inner feeling of being guided by a force outside the mind. The ancient Greeks believed inspiration came from the Muses. Norse mythology ascribes inspiration to the gods. In Hebrew religions, inspiration has divine origins, and in Christianity, it is a gift of the Holy Spirit.

Whether inspiration comes from within or without, it is transcendent, uncontrollable, and irresistible, and most people have experienced it.

> *"It's kind of a revelation."*
>
> *"A sudden realization of something."*
>
> *"Like a little light bulb turning on in my head."*
>
> *"That moment when everything clicks."*
>
> *"I didn't know, and then in an instant, I got it."*
>
> *"The answer came fully formed."*
>
> *"I have this moment of clarity when things just make sense."*

For some, inspiration is an unconscious burst of creativity in a literary, musical, or artistic undertaking or a sudden insight about an invention or scientific principle. For others, it is an internally generated, motivational feeling, accompanied with peak emotions of gratitude, longing, and rightness.

With inspiration comes a feeling of elevation, a surge of energy, and a sudden awareness of greater possibilities. New and better understanding is accompanied with a feeling that you might be more capable than you thought.

Do any of these sound familiar?

> *"The feeling is magical."*
>
> *"One of the most incredible experiences you can have."*
>
> *"There is a sudden understanding–of knowing something in a brand-new way."*
>
> *"It's that moment when you have the courage to step outside your comfort zone."*
>
> *"Unlike motivational speeches, the feeling doesn't go away. It drives me."*
>
> *"That moment when your heart starts beating a little bit faster and you get goose bumps."*

An associate explained it this way: "When I feel inspired, I find myself doing more work with an unforced, positive state of mind. I practice more, study more, replace bad habits, take more risks, and overcome negative thoughts and situations. Not only that, my mood also changes because I am more focused, optimistic, and happy."

Inspired work stands apart from anything else in normal life. Consider Socrates, Einstein, Curie, Mozart, Galileo, or Angelou. An inspired person isn't driven by a desire for money or awards or status. He or she is driven intrinsically by the work itself. The work takes hold of them, guides, molds, and changes them.

People acting on an inspired idea often feel that some greater power than themselves is working through them.

Psychologists Todd M. Thrash and Andrew J. Elliot have studied the physiology of inspiration and *Aha! Moments* and have noted these core aspects of the experience:

First, inspiration comes spontaneously without intention. Regardless of the need, you can't force an *Aha! Moment*. It comes on its own.

Second, inspiration transcends our baser, self-serving concerns and our self-imposed limitations. Such transcendence often involves a moment of clarity and a keen awareness of new possibilities. As Thrash and Elliot note, "The heights of human motivation spring from the beauty and goodness that precede us and awaken us to better possibilities."[6] This moment of clarity is often vivid and can take the form of a grand vision or of "seeing" something that has not been seen before.

Finally, inspiration involves internalized motivation in which the individual strives to transmit, express, or bring into reality a new idea or vision.

- *Inspired individuals report having a stronger drive to master their work but are less competitive in their accomplishments.*
- *Inspired people are more intrinsically motivated and less extrinsically motivated. This motivation strongly impacts work performance.*
- *Inspired people report higher levels of self-esteem, work mastery, creativity, and optimism. Inspired people have uncommon confidence in their own abilities.*[7]

Inspiration is not the same as motivation. Motivation is a general desire or willingness to do something or to act in a particular way. You may feel you need to get yourself motivated to do something you don't want to do, like make that sales call or compile that budget report, clean the house or write a proposal.

Motivation is all about push. Inspiration is all about pull. Motivation is outside in. Inspiration is inside out. Motivation is often fleeting, sometimes inauthentic, and rarely transformational. "Inspiration is about being *called* to act because you're in direct alignment with the magnetic, luminous marrow of potential that is you."[8] Inspiration lies in the center of the soul, potential aching, longing to sprout and grow.

When we are inspired, we are eager to act because of how it makes us feel. Inspiration isn't concrete or permanent. It is most often fleeting, which is why we might think of it as a rush of wind or a flash of light. Inspiration gives us courage to risk our comfort zones and strive for something truly great.

CONSIDER THIS BIG IDEA

Think about a time you had an inspired idea or an Aha! Moment that deeply impacted how you see things or how you feel about something important.

- *What was that moment like?*
- *How did it make you feel?*
- *How has that insight affected how you interact with others?*
- *How has it impacted your work?*

Grab your journal and write about it. For the next week, keep track of inspirational experiences, no matter how small. Pay attention to how you feel when something inspires you.

CHAPTER 2

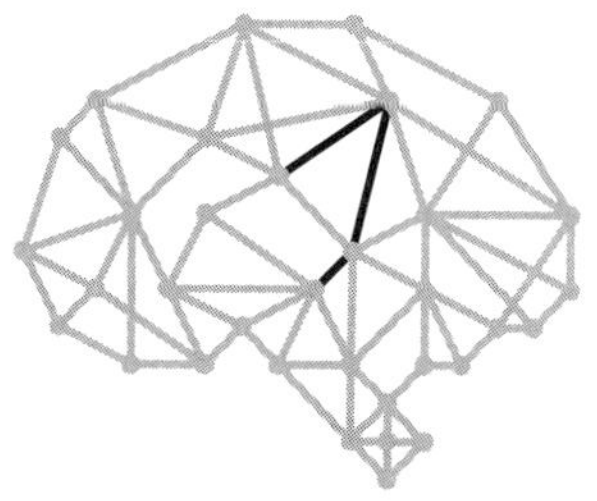

STUCK

"What if you were always stuck in one place, your mind spinning and unable to go forward like tires clenched in mud, because the answers wouldn't reveal themselves to you?"
–Will Lavender

LIZ MURRAY WAS BORN INTO an exceptionally poor family in New York City in 1980. When she was just a toddler, her parents would go into the filthy kitchen of their tiny apartment and, "put the needles in their arms and come out different...their eyes would be flung wide open...it was like electricity was surging through them...they'd pace the apartment, frantic...and then inevitably, the drugs would wear off, and they would crash, and then they would go into their suffering, withdrawal, and the process would repeat itself."[9] Liz and her sister would live in these horrific conditions for the next dozen years.

Liz's mother spent the last few years of her life in a welfare hospital, and her father died of AIDS in a homeless shelter. At the tender age of fifteen, Liz found herself living on the streets, stealing food to survive, begging for money from passersby. Homeless, broke, and uneducated, she was stuck and had no idea what to do.

Have you ever been stuck—we mean really stuck with a problem that feels impossible to fix? Do you find yourself in a situation that seems to be getting worse? Is your creativity stifled to the point of paralysis? Do you feel like you're unable to move, to progress, to get out? You may be stuck in a suffocating job or living with a financial mess that's holding you hostage. You might be pinned in a repressive relationship or an addictive lifestyle with destructive friends and failing health. Are you paying the price for years of neglect and poor choices that seem overwhelming?

Are you stuck?

NO ONE LIKES TO BE STUCK

Even if your problems aren't life or death like Liz Murray's or Archimedes', being stuck has a profound effect on your health, your well-being, and your progress. No one likes to be stuck.

Gerard Puccio at the International Center for Creativity Studies at Buffalo State describes a problem as the "gap between what someone has and what they want."[10] Problems are as ubiquitous and inescapable as traffic on I-405 North in Los Angeles. They are a constant and unpleasant part of life, as predictable as the tides or the rising sun. Every person who has ever lived has had a life full of problems, and each of us has a unique combination of problems that sets us apart from everyone else.

Most problems that occupy our time and make us irritable are merely annoyances. The car has a flat. The dishwasher breaks. The contact won't return the call. Most of these kinds of problems can be fixed with patience, time, or money.

Other problems are overwhelmingly difficult.

For the last ten years, Craig has gone to the local jail twice a week to teach classes to the inmates. He is constantly amazed at the complexity of their lives and their seeming inability to address the challenges they face. A good number of these inmates haven't the skills, mental capability, background, or outside support systems to successfully resolve their enormous problems. Fixing their lives, improving their futures, controlling their anti-social behavior is almost impossible.

We hate problems because they hurt. They cause us pain. But pain is useful if it brings us greater wisdom or warns us that something needs fixing. Our need for Big Ideas comes from the desire to solve or avoid problems. There is a tremendous need in all our lives for creativity, inspired ideas, and better solutions.

The great thing about problems is they are often the catalyst for progress. The desire to fix problems is what stimulates creativity. The world is a better place today than it was a hundred years ago primarily because of last century's problems. It will be better tomorrow for the same reason.

In Paris in the early 1800s, three-year old Louis accidentally blinded himself while playing in his father's workshop. At that time, the blind were considered helpless, and many sightless people ended up begging on the streets.

By the time Louis was a teenager, he was attending a special school for the blind, where he was an accomplished musician and a brilliant student. Still, he was frustrated with

THE GREAT THING ABOUT PROBLEMS IS THEY ARE OFTEN THE CATALYST FOR PROGRESS. THE DESIRE TO FIX PROBLEMS IS WHAT STIMULATES CREATIVITY.

the cumbersome system used to teach blind students to read. Special books with raised lettering had been created for the blind, but to read a book, they had to carefully trace their fingers around each letter. It was a painstaking process that required several minutes to read a single sentence.

Louis was determined to find a better way. He experimented with a system of raised dots and dashes the military had developed, but his schoolmates found the method too difficult. One day, while on vacation at his parents' home, Louis visited his father's leather shop and picked up a blunt awl. The idea came to him in a flash of inspiration. Just as an awl marked leather, he could use a series of raised dots on paper to create an alphabet.

Louis Braille opened up a whole new world for those who couldn't see. In 1878, the World Congress for the Blind voted to make Braille's invention the international reading and writing system for the blind. Braille has now been adopted in almost every language on the planet, impacting tens of millions of people for good.[11]

Before Archimedes had his "Eureka!" moment, how many people had taken a bath and watched the water rise when they got in the tub? The problem he was struggling with served as the catalyst for his profound insight. His high-stakes question (How do I figure out if the crown is pure gold?) combined with the rising water in the tub caused independent neurons in his brain to fire, to reach out and make new connections.

An insightful thought came to Archimedes, and the principle of displacement was refined and applied for a useful purpose.

Problems drive questions, and questions draw out solutions. Problems force thinking and action where they are needed and don't exist.

- *"No good land left and the king won't let us worship the way we want? We'll find a place with plenty of land away from the religion of the king to worship as we see fit."*
- *"The Pony Express is too slow? We'll create the telegraph and the radio and the telephone."*
- *"People are starving? We'll discover ways to grow higher-yield crops on less land for less money."*

By their very nature, problems challenge us, stretch us, and make us stronger. They give us broader perspective and allow us to see with greater clarity. They teach us compassion, empathy, and understanding, and provide opportunities for us to serve and love each another. And they force us to access latent intelligence that can be uncovered in no other way.

You don't have to be stuck. There is a problem-solving model based on thousands of years of Big Ideas. The most prolific and profound thinkers, change agents, and problem solvers throughout history have used a similar model for finding solutions to their most difficult problems.

There is a physiological process for receiving inspiration, the kind of inspiration that provides answers to people's most pressing business issues, creative obstacles, and personal problems. Research says that those who know how to use their brains to access these solutions enjoy happier, more productive, and more fulfilling lives.

LIZ MURRAY

What happened to Liz Murray, the homeless fifteen-year-old girl? In her book, *Breaking Night: A Memoir of Forgiveness, Survival, and My Journey from Homeless to Harvard*, Murray tells how she decided to change her life one night after a penetrating discussion with a friend.

I made a list:

Things to Look Forward to When I Eventually Get a Place:

1. *Privacy*
2. *Being warm all the time*
3. *Food, any time I want*
4. *A big bed!!!*
5. *Clean clothes, socks especially!*
6. *Sleeping and no one wakes me up*
7. *Warm baths*

As she wrote, she had a rush of insight. In order to make any of these things a reality, she needed to graduate from high school.

I tapped my journal's empty page again and wrote:

> *Number of credits required for graduation from high school: 40?... 42? (find this out)*
>
> *My age when the next school year will begin: 17*
>
> *My current address: Wherever I am staying at the moment*
>
> *My current total of high school credits: 1*[12]

That night, Murray made the decision to earn her high school diploma in spite of the odds against her. In the weeks that followed, she was rejected by every school she applied to but one, where she was scheduled for an interview that didn't seem promising. The interview was across town, and she had only enough money for either a subway token or a slice of pizza. Discouraged, cold, and hungry, Murray desperately wanted the pizza, but an unusual prompting told her to go the interview. What if this school accepted her?

Ignoring her empty stomach, she bought the token. At the interview, she met Perry Weiner, founder of the Humanities Preparatory Academy, who accepted her on the condition that he would be her mentor through school. Under Weiner's strict guidance, Murray earned four years of credits in two years with an A average, all while living in New York City parks, stairwells, and subway stations.

Through mind-boggling grit and determination, Murray continued her schooling. With a New York Times scholarship for needy students, she attended and graduated from Harvard University. Murray is now a motivational speaker and has appeared at events alongside former British Prime Minister Tony Blair and his Holiness, the Dalai Lama.

CONSIDER THIS BIG IDEA

Most of the amazing inventions and successful ventures in the world have come as solutions to problems. While we may sometimes feel overwhelmed by our problems, consider a shift in thinking. Recognize that problems are assets waiting to be harvested.

- *Life's problems, big or small, are full of wisdom and intelligence that can be gleaned to enrich our lives.*
- *Actively look for the lessons you can learn from dealing with and solving problems.*
- *Be grateful for the learning opportunities problems present.*
- *As overwhelming as a problem seems, it is usually temporary and much smaller than you might think. Randy Orison wisely said, "No problem is as bad as it seems when it first arrives."*
- *Use the Big Ideas Model you'll read about in this book to find solutions.*

CHAPTER 3

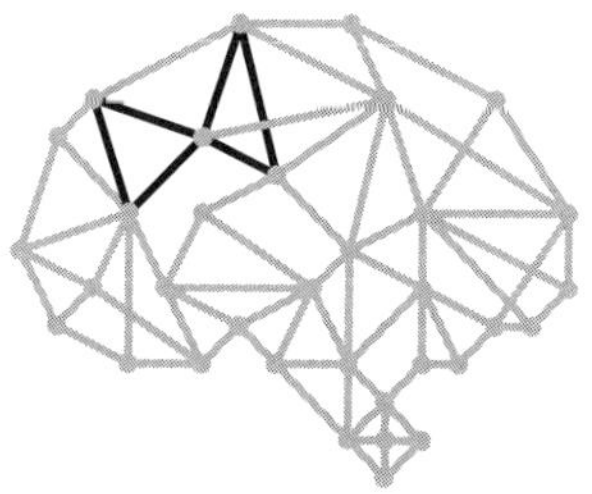

THREE MINDS

"In each of us there is another whom we do not know."
–Carl Jung

AMERICAN SINGER-SONGWRITER TOM WAITS WAS driving down the freeway in Los Angeles when a snippet of a beautiful melody popped into his head. He panicked because he didn't have a piece of paper. He didn't have his tape recorder, a pen, or a pencil. He had no way to capture the melody that had come to him seemingly from out of nowhere.

He started to panic that he wouldn't be able to catch the song–that feeling artists have they're going to miss something. He looked up at the sky and said, "Excuse me, can you not see that I'm driving? If you're serious about wanting to exist, come back and see me in the studio. I spend six hours a day there. You know where to find me. At my piano. Otherwise, go bother somebody else."[13]

Where did that melody come from, and why couldn't Tom Waits hold onto it?

Songwriter, poet, and novelist Leonard Cohen said, "If I knew where inspiration came from, I would go there more often."[14]

According to Albert Einstein, the work and discoveries of Scottish mathematician James Clerk Maxwell (1831–1879) were the "most profound and the most fruitful that physics has experienced since the time of Newton." Maxwell's discoveries helped usher in the era of modern physics, laying the foundation for such fields as special relativity and quantum mechanics. In a survey of a hundred prominent physicists, Maxwell was voted the third greatest physicist of all time, behind only Newton and Einstein.[15]

In 1862, Maxwell developed a set of fundamental equations that unified electricity and magnetism. On his deathbed seventeen years later, Maxwell made an unusual confession, declaring that he did not discover the famous equations he wrote. Rather they came from "something within him."[16] He didn't know how those ideas actually came to him. He said they simply arrived, almost out of thin air.

For Maxwell, the first step in scientific thought was "conscious ignorance...the prelude to every real advance in science." He acknowledged a deeper wisdom that existed independent of his consciousness.

In his bestselling book *Blink,* Malcolm Gladwell describes an experiment at the University of Iowa where participants were given four decks of cards: two red, two blue. They were instructed to turn over one card at a time, and each time, they either won some money or lost some. What they didn't know was all the decks were stacked. Participants could win big money by choosing red, but more often, they lost everything. The blue decks provided a steady series of modest payoffs with significantly fewer losses.

How long did it take the players in the study to figure out that the blue deck was a better bet for winning money?

After fifty cards, a majority of the players developed a "hunch" or a "gut feeling" that the red deck was less desirable and started choosing the blue deck. At that point, most participants could not explain why they started choosing cards exclusively from the blue deck, but after pulling about eighty cards, they understood consciously that the blue deck was stacked for better, more consistent payoffs.

The players in the experiment were hooked up to machines that track sweat glands in the palms as well as skin temperature. This test, the Galvanic Skin Response, measures stress and nervousness. After only ten cards were drawn, the Iowa scientists began detecting stress when players chose from the red deck, forty cards before they had a "hunch" and seventy cards before they consciously figured out the game.[17]

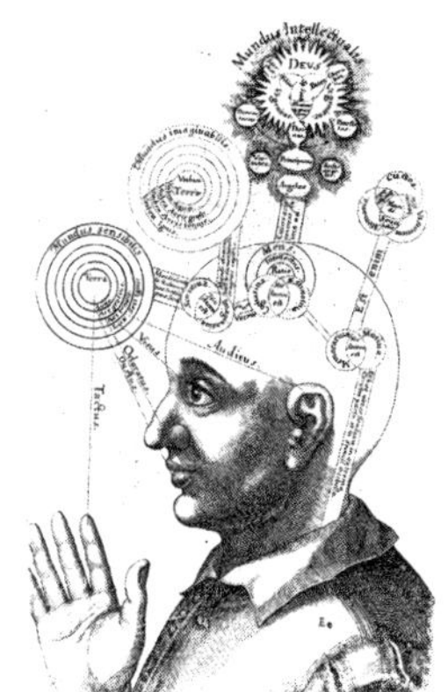

Gladwell proposes that there is a second kind of brain, or mind, operating below the surface capable of quickly making sophisticated judgments.

WHAT IS CONSCIOUSNESS?

Consciousness is active thought. It is awareness. It is a stream of thinking, more or less constant, going on inside your head. It is the pain you feel when you hit your thumb with a hammer. It is the joy of seeing a sunset or the sadness of parting with a loved one. The five senses are often experienced in consciousness. Consciousness is the emotions you feel, the thoughts you think, and the awareness you have of your surroundings.

But consciousness is not the only thing going on inside your head.

Clinical psychologist Warren W. Tyron says the idea of "another mind" independent of one's consciousness is at least two thousand years old. The Greek physician Galen (130–210) proposed that people make unconscious inferences from their perceptions. It was believed that through the unconscious that the Muses communicated to and influenced humans.[18]

The idea of more than one mind was also suggested by Roman philosopher Plotinus and Christian philosopher St Augustine (354–430), who likened the unconscious mind to a "ghost that is experienced as a felt presence, only invisible."[19]

Saint Thomas Aquinas (1225–1274) observed that common behaviors and habits like nail biting, spontaneous laughter, or tapping out a rhythm with one's foot have no connection to people's general awareness. He put all such actions in a category separate from other acts "since they do not proceed from the deliberation of the reason."[20]

Four hundred years later, Gottfried Wilhelm Leibniz (1646–1716) suggested that the mind is a combination of both accessible and inaccessible parts and proposed that things go on in the brain of which we are not aware. He called these events "petite perceptions" and believed there are strivings and tendencies we are not aware of but that nonetheless affect our behavior. This was the first significant commentary on unconscious urges, and Leibniz conjectured that his ideas would be critical to explaining why humans behave as they do.[21]

THE THREE MINDS

You may have a sense of what the words conscious, subconscious, and unconscious mean, but because they are so important to understanding how the mind works, we would like to give each of them a detailed definition.

Sigmund Freud (1856–1939) popularized the ideas of both the subconscious and the unconscious.[22] He proposed a three-level mind model:

1. **Conscious mind**: *The feelings, actions, and thoughts within one's awareness.*
   Feelings *such as awe at an ocean vista, thirst and the need for a drink, or irritation at a family member.*
   Actions *such as hiking up a hill, playing the piano, feeding the baby, or hammering a nail.*
   Thoughts *such as developing a plot for your next novel, planning a vacation, or working out a math problem.*
2. **Subconscious mind**: *The reactions and automatic actions we become aware of only when we think about them. Habits live in the subconscious mind.*

   When we drive to work, we tend to follow the same route, and the need for decision-making is almost non-existent. After a few days of travel, the journey becomes routine, and we hardly pay attention as we commute. At that point, we drive with the subconscious mind. The only time we have to think about the process is when something out of the ordinary happens. Depending on how much focus you give to these activities, they might also fall under subconscious thinking: taking a shower, putting on your makeup, vacuuming the house, breathing, watching TV, reacting to stress, and eating.

   According to Nobel prize-winning psychologist Daniel Kahneman, the brain has a limited pool of cognitive resources known as "attention."[23] Not all tasks require equal amounts of attention. Doing physics homework, teaching a child her letters, or repairing a watch require a great deal of attention. If we don't bring our conscious focus to these tasks, we'll make mistakes. But other activities, like driving or eating, don't require much mental effort, which is how habits are formed.

3. **Unconscious mind**: *The past events and memories and most of the present work that takes place in our brain that is inaccessible, no matter how hard we try to retrieve it.*

   The unconscious mind influences judgment, feelings, and behavior. Our urges, intuitions, dreams, and snap decisions all originate in the unconscious. The vast majority of our bodily functions are also managed by the unconscious mind, such as blood pressure, body temperature, the digestion of food, the healing of a wound, and many others that are far too complex for the conscious mind to direct.

These three minds make up three distinct levels of consciousness. While we are fully aware of what is going on in the conscious mind and can access the subconscious with some effort, we are unsure of the specific nature of the information stored in the unconscious mind. The unconscious mind harbors thoughts, memories, and emotions apart from conscious thought.

Freud compared these three minds to an iceberg. The ten percent you can access is the conscious and subconscious, and the much larger part under the water is the unconscious. A hundred years after Freud's analysis, scientists are still struggling for understanding about unconsciousness. Unlike the heart or lungs, the unconscious mind can't be empirically studied or directly seen, examined, or measured.

Subsequent research has broadened Freud's theory on the unconscious mind. There is evidence that the vast majority of the mind's collective thought takes place at the unconscious level.

THE UNCONSCIOUS MIND

Although we can't see it, many studies confirm that the unconscious mind does exist. Researchers at Columbia University Medical Center discovered that fleeting images of fearful faces—images that appear and disappear so quickly they escape conscious awareness—generate anxiety that can be detected in the brain with the latest neuroimaging machines.[24]

The unconscious is the driver of all the mental activity you don't consciously manage, activity such as feelings, automatic skills, unnoticed perceptions, fleeting thoughts, reactions, phobias, passions, and desires. The unconscious is the storehouse of wisdom and forgotten memories, the home and the assembler of night dreams. When you go to bed with a problem on your mind and wake up the following morning with the solution, that's the unconscious mind at work.

Craig recently purchased a sleeveless down-filled jacket. Attached to the jacket was small bag made of the same material as the jacket. He had no idea what the bag was for but put it in his sock drawer and promptly forgot about it. Weeks later, he had a dream where he observed himself stuffing the jacket into the small bag. When he awoke, he got the jacket and the bag, and just like in his dream, the jacket fit perfectly inside the bag. Even though his conscious brain had completely forgotten about the bag, his unconscious brain had not. It solved the problem and sent the information to the conscious mind via a dream.

The unconscious appears to be the place in the mind where thoughts and ideas are born and where Aha! Moments and Big Ideas originate. Most information processing resides outside of consciousness for reasons of efficiency. The mind operates best by relegating a significant degree of high level, sophisticated processing to the unconscious.[25]

That is probably what happened to Tom Waits while he was driving in Los Angeles traffic. Because his mind wasn't focused on anything on particular, his unconscious mind sent him a new melody.

We can't force the unconscious mind to reveal itself or release its vast expanse of knowledge, wisdom, brilliance, and memory. "[It] cannot be ordered about," says philosopher William Irvine. "You can't, for example, wake up one morning and say, 'Unconscious mind, today I want to prove Goldbach's Conjecture,' one of the great unsolved problems of mathematics. On hearing this request your unconscious mind will simply laugh—not that you realize it is doing so. What you must instead do is interest your unconscious mind in working on a problem by working on it with your conscious mind. It might take hours, days, or even weeks of unsuccessful conscious effort before your unconscious mind even takes an interest. You will know it has because you will start to experience *Aha! Moments* with respect to the problem."[26]

You must know how to use all three minds effectively if you want to have more Aha! Moments or Big Ideas. The Big Ideas Model you'll learn about in this book uses all three minds to generate bigger and better ideas.

Let the discovery begin!

PART TWO

GOING DEEPER INTO BRAIN SCIENCE

CHAPTER 4

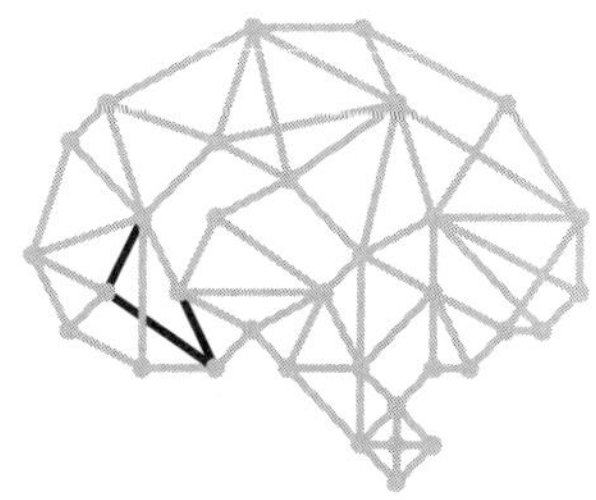

BRAINWAVES

"There exists a microscopic breed of brain beetle, commonly known as an 'idea.' An idea desires only one thing: To catch the perfect brainwave."
–Leah Broadby

THE ALARM WAKES JASON WITH a start from an unsettled sleep. With a groan, he presses the snooze button. He *hates* mornings, especially Monday mornings.

Yesterday around four in the afternoon, like every other Sunday he can remember, his head started to ache and his gut tightened when the football game ended. The weekend had wound down, and another exhausting week was about to start all over again.

If Jason doesn't get up immediately, he'll miss the 5:40 AM train and be late for work again—a bad habit the boss frequently reminds him about. He slides out of bed, showers, drinks two cups of strong coffee, and with the thrill and lightness of a garden slug, drags himself to the train station.

Like many of us, Jason has a bucket full of problems, and they're getting worse. He's deeply in debt and seems to get further in the hole every year. Occasionally, he's given a small raise at work, but no matter how much money he makes, the government or the kids or his wife takes it. Or the house or the cars need repairs. Or the credit card companies want their cut.

Jason dreads going to work. He feels stuck in a dead-end job with no room for advancement and no recognition of his hard work, which has been slacking recently. The boss stifles his creativity, and his coworkers don't seem to care that he's too busy to give his full attention to group projects.

Jason's personal life is a mess. He has no time for meaningful, relationship-building conversations or activities with his kids. They're becoming increasingly distant and increasingly unavailable. He barely speaks to his wife because it takes too much energy to communicate, and he doesn't know how to deal with disagreements. He and his wife usually end up yelling at each other and not solving anything.

What is going on with Jason?

THE MAGNIFICENT BRAIN

At the root of all our thoughts, emotions, and behaviors is the electrical and chemical communication that takes place in the neurons in our brains. There are approximately one hundred billion neurons and ten times as many glial cells in our brains. **Neurons** are cells that process and transmit information using electrical impulses. The electricity in your brain could power a twenty-watt bulb. These signals transition from one neuron to the other via specialized connections called synapses. Synapses, in turn, transmit information among the neurons with over one thousand unique proteins called neurotransmitters.[27] Through these synaptic connections, each neuron is linked to ten thousand other neurons. When our synapses are firing in harmony, they create a synchronized neural network linked to a specific state of consciousness, thought, and mood.

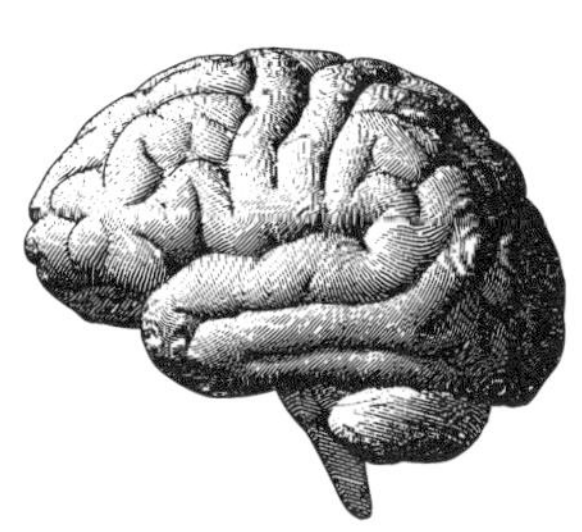

According to neuroscientist David Eagleman, "The cells are connected to one another in a network of such staggering complexity that it bankrupts human language and necessitates new strains of mathematics. A typical neuron makes about ten thousand connections to neighboring neurons. Given the billions of neurons, this means there are as many connections in a single cubic centimeter of brain tissue as there are stars in the Milky Way galaxy."[28]

Physicist Michio Kaku says the human brain "is the most complicated object in the known Universe."[29]

BRAINWAVES

The combination of synchronized electrical activity is called brainwave activity because of the wave-like patterns it creates as the brain does its work. These brainwaves can be detected and measured using an electroencephalogram (EEG), which measures wave levels throughout the brain. Neurologists have identified five types of brainwaves. From slowest to fastest, they are:

Delta: .1 – 4 Hz, deep dreamless sleep

Theta: 4 – 7 Hz, deep relaxation, meditation, REM sleep

Alpha: 8 – 12 Hz, relaxed, calm, lucid, daydreaming

Beta: 12 – 40 Hz, awake, normal alert consciousness

Gamma: 40 Hz, peak performance, flow, Aha! Moments

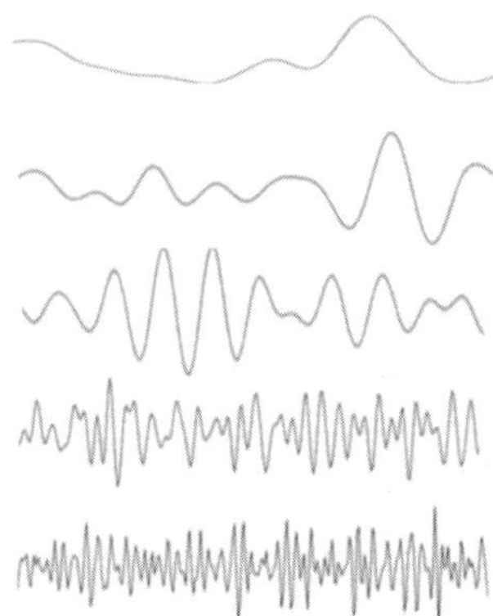

Delta: *Delta brainwaves have the slowest frequency, typically .1 to 4 cycles per second. When you're in deep, dreamless sleep, your brain produces delta brainwaves.*

Theta: *Theta brainwaves range from 4 to 7 cycles per second. When you're sleeping and dreaming, your brain is producing theta brainwaves.*

Alpha: *Alpha brainwaves are faster than theta, ranging from 8 to 12 cycles per second. When you have completed a task and sit down to rest, you are most likely in a daydreaming, alpha state. When you ponder, meditate, or take a leisurely stroll, you are usually in an alpha state.*

Beta: *Beta brainwaves are faster than alpha, ranging from 12 to 40 cycles per second. When you are engaged in conscious mental activities, in conversation, or actively listening, beta waves dominate. Beta waves are characteristics of a strongly engaged mind.*

Gamma: *Gamma brainwaves are the fastest brainwaves, moving at a rate of 40 to 90 cycles per second. Gamma brainwave production involves the entire brain, tends to be short-lived, and is associated with moments of increased awareness, heightened consciousness, and intellectual acuity. A gamma spike* *is a momentary production of gamma brainwaves that takes place shortly before you experience an Aha! Moment or a Big Idea.*

Like Jason, most people experience all five types of brainwaves during a twenty-four-hour period. When we are awake, all five types of brainwaves might be active, but one brainwave state is dominant at any given time.

The brain works optimally by shifting from one dominant brainwave state to another every few hours. Even when we dream, our brains transition every ninety minutes or so, back and forth among alpha, the slower theta, and the even slower delta state. If we stay in one primary brain state for too long, we become exhausted, anxious, lethargic, or we simply fall asleep.

CHAPTER 5

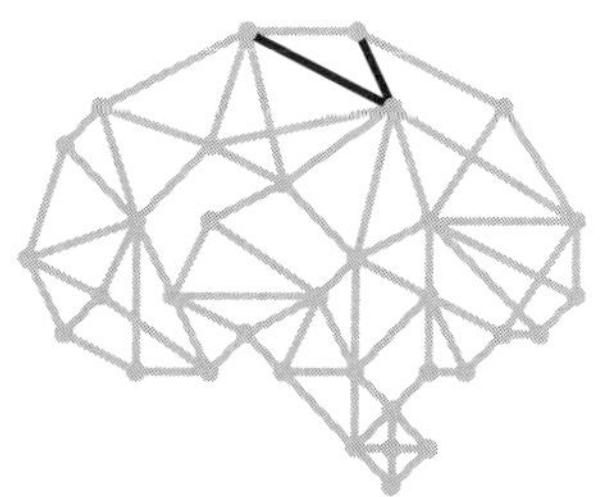

BETA: THE WORKING BRAIN

"You have to work hard to get your thinking clean to make it simple. But it's worth it in the end because once you get there, you can move mountains."
–Steve Jobs

THE BETA BRAIN IS THE CONSCIOUS, working brain.

The beta brain:

- *gathers information*
- *makes decisions*
- *deals with problems*
- *pays focused attention*
- *gets things done*

Beta brainwaves are the primary brainwaves when we are involved in activities that require focused attention, critical thinking, communicating, problem solving, and mental exertion—the kinds of things many people do all day on their jobs.

The very act of opening his eyes in the morning increases Jason's beta brainwaves. He habitually drinks two cups of coffee to get his brain going. The caffeine causes a boost in beta activity, and he functions with increased energy and mental focus.

Jason's brain often stays in beta throughout the day. His job in customer service dealing with annoyed people requires high energy, keen problem-solving skills, and prolonged mental alertness. To stay attentive, Jason consumes an energy drink and takes a nootropic or "smart pill" in the morning. Like the coffee, the energy drink and smart pill increase his beta activity. They make him feel good, and people in the office like his rapid thinking, quick wit, extraordinary memory, and assertive manner—classic signs of a person with high beta activity.

Beta waves have a stimulating *and* exhausting effect on the brain and the body. Following lunch, Jason is both anxious and irritable. Although he doesn't exercise, his muscles are sore. He has a tension headache along with persistent heartburn. To address these symptoms, he guzzles antacids and headache medicine.

Have you ever felt completely exhausted after a long day of thinking and problem solving? That's the way Jason feels almost every night as he rides the train home. He's worn out, but all he did was sit at his desk and take care of other people's problems.

FUELING THE BRAIN

Even if Jason isn't active physically, his beta brain works hard. It takes a lot of fuel to keep the brain functioning in beta mode. Although our brains are only two percent of our body weight, they use 70 percent of our daily intake of glucose, 25 percent of the oxygen, and 20 percent of the calories we consume.[30] The more time we spend in beta mode, the more fuel our brains use. No wonder Jason is exhausted at the end of the day.

The first thing Jason does when he gets home is pour himself a strong drink. Alcohol is a depressant, but it's also an indirect stimulant. It affects Jason's excitatory neurotransmitters as well as his inhibitory neurotransmitters by altering the chemical messengers that control his thought processes, behaviors, and emotions.

Alcohol suppresses the release of glutamate, resulting in a slowdown along his brain's highways. His thoughts, speech, and movements are sluggish, and the more he drinks, the more of these effects he feels. Alcohol also increases the release of dopamine in the brain's reward center, a group of neural structures responsible for all pleasurable activity. By increasing the dopamine levels in his brain, alcohol tricks Jason into thinking he feels good so he keeps drinking to trigger the release of more dopamine. At the same time, he's triggering other brain chemicals that make him feel depressed.

WE INTERRUPT THIS CHAPTER TO TALK ABOUT INTERRUPTIONS

Poet Samuel Taylor Coleridge (1772–1834) tells of falling asleep in a chair when he was staying at a farmhouse near Porlock, a small village in southwest England. He had been reading about the extravagances of Mongolian general Kubla Khan's palace and had a vivid dream wherein he was given the words of a poem.

Coleridge writes of this event in the third person. "On awakening he appeared to himself to have a distinct recollection of the whole and taking his pen, ink, and paper, instantly and eagerly wrote down the lines that are preserved. 'In Xanadu, did Kubla Khan/A stately pleasure dome decree....'"

But after he wrote these words, Coleridge was "called out by a person from Porlock on business and detained by him above an hour."

That interruption proved devastating. Upon Coleridge's return, he realized to his horror that though he still retained some vague and dim recollection of the general theme, with the exception of some eight or ten scattered lines and images, all the rest had passed away "like the images on the surface of a stream into which a stone has been cast." As a result, "Kubla Khan" is only 54 lines long and remains, by Coleridge's account, unfinished.

Interruptions surround us. Whether it's a knock at the door, an incoming text message, or a notification on our cell phone, interruptions keep our brains operating in beta mode, virtually halting the creative process.

INFORMATION OVERLOAD

One of the realities of our time is the vast amount of information available on an endless array of technological devices we carry with us everywhere we go. We have unlimited access to the flow of new and interesting information, and many of us want it all.

In his book *Critical Path*, futurist and inventor R. Buckminster Fuller (1895–1983) created the "Knowledge Doubling Curve," hypothesizing that until 1900, human knowledge doubled about every century. By the end of World War II, knowledge was doubling every twenty-five years. Today, nanotechnology advances double every two years and clinical knowledge every eighteen months. On average, human knowledge is doubling every thirteen months. According to IBM, the build-out of the "internet of things" has led to the doubling of knowledge every 12 hours![31] Most of this information finds its way to the Internet as quickly as it is discovered.

We are, quite literally, drowning in information, information that fragments our attention and keeps our brains in an agitated beta state. The consequences are startling.

We spend most of our waking hours in beta mode because that is when new information arrives to our conscious mind. The beta state is for information gathering. But the information doesn't come in distinct, organized packets, nor is it put in the same place in the brain when it arrives. Once information appears, primarily through the senses, it is sent to various areas of the brain, waiting for organization.

Activities such as fishing, gardening, meditating, or taking a quiet stroll through the park provide the brain with the rest needed to do its job most effectively. We will elaborate on this in a later chapter. Without this rest, the brain still functions, but it works harder and with less efficiency, like an automobile engine with half the spark plugs missing. Many of us have operated this way for so long, we think it's normal and have no idea what it's like to think with a fully charged brain.

Considerable research confirms that your brain works best when it regularly transitions from faster to slower brain states every few hours. But we live in a time where mental "down-shifting" takes place only when we're on vacation or when we are exhausted at the end of a long day. Interruptions and distractions from our tech tools tend to keep us in a high beta state.

THE TECHNOLOGY CHALLENGE

Jason is not only addicted to alcohol but to anything that has a screen, like his TV, his computer, his tablet, and his cell phone, which never leaves his side.

For all their incalculable benefits, smartphones, social media, and the Internet are intentionally designed to distract and interrupt us. Anyone who has been online has experienced the following scenario: You fire up the web browser to do some research and notice you have seven unread emails. While answering emails, Facebook prompts you to wish happy birthday to two friends. After you've read three articles and all the comments on your Facebook newsfeed, you have to update some information on Instagram. You then notice a new recipe you want to try and two more articles to read. Then your sister shares photos of her new grandson, and you soon go to Pinterest to check out kitchen remodels. Three hours later, you're on Twitter reading commentary on the latest Avengers movie. This experience is much like walking into a room and forgetting why you're there. On the Internet, there is no end to the rooms you can enter, and most of them have no connection to the one you were just in. Interruptions are never ending, and it's easy to get lost.

Online distraction is particularly challenging for young adults and teens. College students check their digital devices, particularly their smartphones, an average of 11.43 times during a 50-minute class period. While in class, 12 percent text, email, or search Google more than 30 times a day.[32]

Such perpetual distraction limits the brain's ability to focus, capture concepts, and learn. During the four years students spend in college classrooms, they may be distracted during classes for as much as two-thirds of a school year. As you might guess, the cost of lost learning is *staggering*.

In *The Shallows–What the Internet is Doing to Our Brains*, researcher Nicholas Carr asks, "Is Google making us stupid?" Try reading a book while doing a crossword puzzle. "That," says Carr, "is the intellectual environment of the Internet."[33]

"The net engages all of our senses, and...it engages them simultaneously." The Internet intentionally keeps you in a high beta state by overwhelming your brain with options and stimuli. The ability to stay focused and concentrate for long periods, a skill that has been developed by humans over tens of thousands of years, is diminishing drastically.

"Neuroscientists and psychologists have discovered that even as adults, our brains are very plastic. They're very malleable, they adapt at the cellular level to whatever we happen to be doing...the more time we spend surfing and skimming and scanning...the more adept we become at that mode of thinking." As a society, we are losing our ability to employ a "slower, more contemplative mode of thought," the kind of thinking that accompanies the alpha state. Because we are losing our ability to focus and to think deeply, "we are becoming less creative in our thinking."[34]

Technology is neither inherently good or bad. If we exercise control and discipline, the Internet's contribution to the quality of our lives is immeasurable. But used without restraint, the Internet has the power to destroy our ability to think creatively.

THE INTERNET HAS THE POWER TO DESTROY OUR ABILITY TO THINK CREATIVELY.

A distracted brain is a dangerous brain, whether it's a preoccupied teen driving while texting, a coworker who thinks he can get more done by multitasking, or a mother who ignores her toddler because she's engrossed in social media. These are realities of our day, and the consequences are frightening.

According to a study done by the Transport Research Laboratory, a texting driver is more dangerous than a drunk driver. Those who drive while reading or composing texts have 35 percent slower reactions times. By comparison, drunk drivers display a 12 percent decrease in reaction time, while drivers intoxicated with cannabis have 21 percent slowed response times.[35]

Jason may think he is productive when he juggles multiple projects at the same time, but the truth is, his brain doesn't work as well, and the work he produces is mediocre. Typical technology distractions in the workplace can temporarily lower a person's I.Q. score by as many as ten points and decrease productivity by as much as 40 percent.[36]

Multiple studies confirm children suffer when their parents pay more attention to their smart phones than to their kids. Such children are more negative and less resilient. They feel unimportant, and their intellectual and emotional development is hampered.[37]

RISE IN ANXIETY

A predictable rise in anxiety accompanies those who spend their waking hours in beta mode. People born between 1995 and 2012 are growing up with their own smartphones, have an Instagram account before they start high school, and don't remember a time before the Internet. They are also growing up frightened, nervous, and increasingly anxious.

According to the National Institute of Mental Health, anxiety is now the most common mental health disorder in the United States, affecting nearly one-third of both adolescents and adults.[38] In just the last decade, anxiety has overtaken depression as the most common reason college students seek counseling services. "Anxious teenagers from all backgrounds are relentlessly comparing themselves with their peers...and the results are almost uniformly distressing."[39]

Research by Dr. Jean Twenge suggests that the use of smartphones correlates with the rise in depression and unhappiness among high school students and college age adults. A number of studies make the connection between social media use and unhappiness. "Teen depression and suicide have skyrocketed since 2011. It's not an exaggeration to describe [the Internet generation] as being on the brink of the worst mental health crisis in decades. Much of this deterioration can be traced to their phones.... There is compelling evidence that the devices we've placed in young people's hands are having profound effects on their lives and making them seriously unhappy."[40]

Heightened physiological responses to anxiety, like headaches, butterflies in the stomach, rapid heartbeat, and labored breathing become habituated as the brain's network patterns thicken and lose their ability to provide mental relief. Without realizing it, many people have parked their brains in beta mode. Some of us have conditioned our brains to steadily produce beta waves and manufacture accompanying brain chemicals. These people live in an unabated state of chronic worry, high anxiety, and stressful thoughts. Chronic stress reduces levels of critical neurotransmitters, especially serotonin and dopamine—naturally produced chemicals that help people feel joy, hope, and happiness.

WHAT TV DOES TO THE BRAIN

Studies have found that the brain's higher functions, like the areas used for analysis and reasoning, go offline when we unwind for an evening in front of the TV.[41] As we mindlessly switch from one channel to the next, watching innumerable commercials designed to excite our minds, the visual cortex, the brain's largest cortical tissue, is highly stimulated. Researcher Megan Neal explains, "This basically leaves the brain in a sort of limbo state of rest—neurons are still firing but the mind is not actually engaged—it's taking in a boatload of information but not processing it, so the brain isn't fully relaxed, but it's not being exercised either."[42] The brain lands in a semi-confused state, not sure what to do.

According to professors Esther Thorson at Michigan State and Annie Lang at Indiana University, the rapidly changing visuals and sudden noises of commercials and many TV shows trigger the brain's "orienting response," an involuntary survival instinct managed by the Reticular Activating System (RAS) to stay alert and monitor any sudden stimuli in the environment. We'll talk more about the RAS later. Many shows and most commercials are specifically shot and edited with the purpose of interrupting thought, inhibiting the brain's ability to consolidate information and make new connections, two of the most important activities of the alpha state.[43]

People who are continually anxious or worried are in a constrained mental state, referred to as being "alpha blocked."[44]

They find it difficult, if not impossible, to slow their brains down, hence the need for relaxants, drugs, and sleeping pills.

TOO MUCH BETA

When Jason is angry, anxious, or worried, it's hard for him to think clearly. In moments of stress, his nervous system responds by releasing extra adrenaline and cortisol, making his heart pound faster, his muscles tighten, and blood pressure rise. These physical changes increase his strength and stamina, enhance his reaction time, and heighten his focus. In these stressful moments, Jason's brain functions are in high beta.

Higher beta frequencies are associated with elevated stress levels. Stress, anxiety, and mental burnout release excessive amounts of **adrenaline** and **cortisol** into the body. Too much adrenaline impairs our sleep and promotes restless leg syndrome. Known as the fight-or-flight hormone, adrenaline contributes to impatience, anger, and general anxiety, which in turn promote the beta brain state. It can be a vicious downward spiral.

An overproduction of cortisol causes weight gain and mood swings and is a factor in low energy and a general lack of enthusiasm for life.

CONSIDER THIS BIG IDEA

For the next week, track how much time you spend worrying about the future. Do you obsess about things you can't control or feel anxious for no apparent reason? Consider what causes these feelings and why. Look for patterns in your thinking. Is your anxiety based in reality?

If you're looking for a better way to unwind at the end of a stressful day or to find better solutions to life's challenges, sleep doctor Matthew Edlund suggests that exercise, meditation, or hanging out with friends is better than TV. "If you combine social and physical activity, you'll feel more stimulated, alert, alive than vegging out in front of TV."[45]

CHAPTER 6

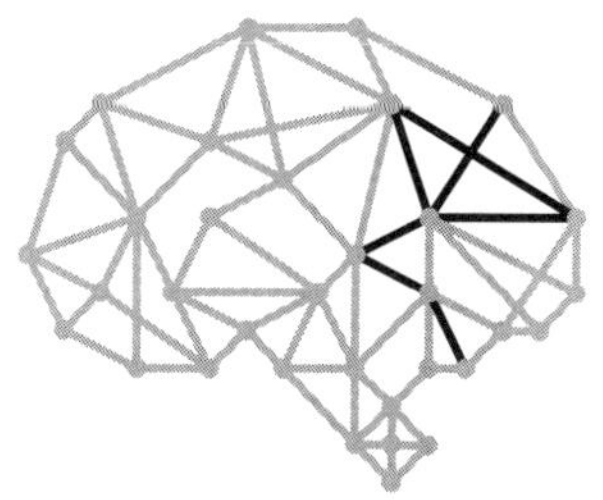

ALPHA: THE RENEWING BRAIN

"A man is not idle because he is absorbed in thought. There is a visible labor and there is an invisible labor."
–Victor Hugo

As Jason fights his way through one battle after another, he notices that Nicole, a co-worker, seems to be happy and at peace on the job. He wonders why she doesn't seem to have the same stress and pressure he does. Her job performance is superior. She accomplishes more in the morning than Jason does all day, and she always shares good ideas in meetings.

Like Jason, Nicole has stress and uncontrollable situations in her life. She is a single mom with two kids, an ailing mother, and a high-pressure job. But unlike Jason, who has taught his brain to stay in beta, Nicole has learned to rest and renew her brain throughout the day. At work, she spends her first fifteen minutes planning before turning on her computer. Every few hours during work, she turns off her cell phone, leaves the building, and walks around the block. Sometimes she closes her door, sits in her chair, and closes her eyes or stares out the window.

SLOWING DOWN

What Jason thinks is wasting time is actually the secret to Nicole's productivity, creativity, and peaceful state of mind. Beta brainwaves accompany an active brain in high gear, but alpha brainwaves are indicative of a calm and relaxed brain. EEG scans show alpha to be the dominant wave generated by those who are actively meditating and are experiencing calm, yet lucid, and "blissful" mental states.[46]

The frontal cortex is the part of the brain involved in problem solving, spontaneity, memory, language, judgment, impulse control, and social behavior. Alpha waves increase and spread throughout the frontal cortex when we close our eyes. Have you ever noticed how closing your eyes helps you think more deeply and find answers to difficult problems? Alpha waves are also dominant immediately before the brain experiences creative insight. Alpha states attend serene, tranquil, and pleasant thinking.

Using a few simple techniques, Nicole has learned how to slow the beta waves in her brain to alpha waves. When she feels anxious and notices her muscles tensing up, rather than reaching for the coffee, she shuts the door to her office, puts her phone on mute, closes her eyes, and practices a simple breathing exercise to raise her energy and relax her body and mind. It takes no more than a minute or two, but it lowers her anxiety and leaves her feeling invigorated. She can think with greater clarity.

BRAIN MINERALS

The neurons in our brains are able to transmit electrical impulses because of potassium and sodium ions that create positive and negative electrical charges in the neurons themselves.[47] After spending a couple of hours in the beta state, the brain's ratio of potassium to sodium ions becomes imbalanced, and our neurons become less efficient at moving the electrical impulses along. The brain's ability to think effectively is diminished. This mineral imbalance is the main cause of what is known as "mental fatigue" or "burnout," which is one of the main reasons Jason is exhausted at the end of the day.

It only takes ten to fifteen minutes in the alpha state—the time it takes Nicole to walk around the block—to restore the sodium and potassium to proper ratios in her brain.

In a study of professional basketball players, neuroscientists found increased alpha brainwave activity in the left side of a player's brain just before he or she makes a basket. Amateur basketball players show an increase in beta activity when they take shots. Additional long-term studies indicate that as players improve their game, they produce more alpha waves, suggesting that alpha brainwaves are indispensable for high-level, peak performance.[48]

MINDFULNESS AND MEDITATION

Slower brainwave production is one of the goals of mindfulness and meditation programs. During meditation, the brain slows down and gets a rest five times deeper than sleep. This deeper rest gives the body and the brain an opportunity to heal.

Meditation helps the right and left hemispheres of the brain communicate with each other by strengthening the corpus callosum, the bridge between the two. This connection allows us to generate creative solutions even in high-stress situations.

Other benefits of regular meditation and mindfulness practices include less anxiety and depression,[49] a lengthened attention span,[50] a reduction in age-related memory loss,[51] an increase in mental sharpness and fluid intelligence in older adults,[52] and decreased sensitivity to pain.[53] Researchers at the University of Washington discovered that mindfulness practices are twice as effective as 12-step programs in preventing drug-addiction relapse.[54]

These many benefits can come from meditating as little as twenty minutes a day.

There is also a fascinating inverse correlation between the time spent in meditation and mindfulness practices and the time required to accomplish other tasks. Those who take time to meditate will find they have more than enough time to complete the rest of the things on their to-do lists.

SLOW THE BRAIN

Some of history's most productive people took regular time to slow their brains and experience the rich rewards of alpha waves.

- *Ben Franklin spent up to an hour a day taking "air baths:" opening the windows, removing his clothes, sitting in a chair, and thinking.*

- *In stressful times, Einstein would row a small boat to the middle of a lake, sit on the water, and do nothing but think, sometimes for hours.*
- *During the darkest hours of World War II, Winston Churchill took most afternoons to relax in a hot tub while he painted.*
- *The Dalai Lama spends between two and three hours a day in various stages of meditation and prayer reflecting on "the roots of compassion and what he can do for his people, the 'Chinese brothers and sisters,' while also preparing himself for his death."*[55]
- *Psychiatrist M. Scott Peck spent up to two and half hours a day doing nothing but thinking and praying. He claimed it was the most productive time of his day.*
- *Arianna Huffington starts her mornings with deep breathing and gratitude. Then she does thirty minutes of meditation and thirty minutes of exercise. She also regularly practices yoga.*[56]

CONSIDER THIS BIG IDEA

With some practice, you can generate stress-relieving alpha waves any time, even during high stress situations. In your journal, keep track of what works best for you. Here are some ideas:

- *With your eyes closed, breathe in deeply. Hold the breath, then let it out slowly. Repeat five or six times and pay attention to how you feel.*
- *Get the* Breethe *app and follow some of the programs.*
- *Take a solitary walk. Leave your cell phone behind.*
- *Engage in an artistic pursuit like painting, sculpting, drawing, writing, or crafting.*

- *Meditate by sitting or lying down on your bed and clearing your mind. Close your eyes and concentrate on your breathing.*
- *Listen to relaxing music.*

CHAPTER 7

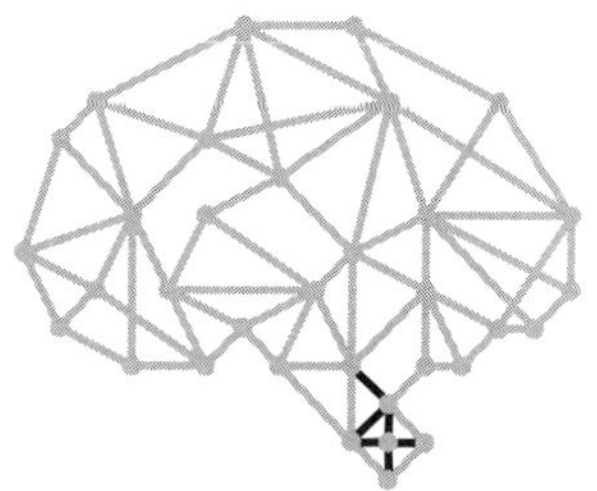

THETA AND DELTA: THE CREATIVE BRAIN

"To sleep. To sleep, perchance to dream."
–William Shakespeare

JUST AS ALPHA WAVES ARE SLOWER than beta waves, theta brainwaves are slower than alpha, and delta are the slowest of all.

When Nicole goes to bed, instead of checking Facebook or watching the news, she reflects on her day and writes a few lines in a gratitude journal. This nightly activity doesn't take much time, but it delivers incredible benefits to Nicole's emotional well-being and helps her brain transition from more active brain states to the slower theta, so she can gently fall asleep and enjoy a peaceful night's rest.

SLEEP

Jason is under the false impression he can function perfectly on less sleep. One of the main reasons he's anxious, irritable, and craving caffeine and alcohol is because of his terrible sleeping habits. His habitual lack of sleep is one of the main reasons he will die much younger than he might have. He has existed on six hours of sleep per night for so long, he thinks his exhaustion, short temper, and irritability are normal.

Nicole feels more alert, more creative, and much happier when she gets at least eight hours of sleep every night. Getting a good night's rest is one of the most important reasons for Nicole's creative and insightful brain.

When Nicole writes for a few minutes before falling sleep, she is generally in a low beta. When she puts the book down, turns off the light, and closes her eyes, her brainwaves immediately slow from beta to alpha. When she falls asleep, her brainwaves go from alpha to theta to delta a few minutes later. Delta waves are up to ten times slower than the beta waves Nicole produces when she is active during the day.

During the course of an eight-hour sleep, our brains continually transition between higher brainwave activity or rapid eye movement sleep (REM) to slower brainwave activity, non-rapid eye movement sleep (NREM). This change takes place about every 90 minutes, as often as four or five times during an eight-hour period. While our brains transition back and forth, they are performing at least two vital tasks: neural harvesting and memory consolidation.

NREM SLEEP AND NEURAL HARVESTING

Although we experience short periods of REM sleep the first half of an eight-hour period, the first four hours are primarily spent in NREM sleep, the deeper sleep where the brain waves slow down considerably. During this slower period, the brain does its neural housecleaning: cutting, clipping, and dissolving the clutter of needless neurons that inhibit the brain and limit creativity and insight.

Neuroscientist Matthew Walker says, "A key function of deep NREM sleep, which predominates early in the night, is to do the work of weeding out and removing unnecessary neural connections."[57]

In addition to neurons, the brain is primarily made up of glial cells that insulate, surround, and support the neurons. Glial cells outnumber neurons by about ten to one. Microglial cells perform essential housecleaning tasks. Like a gardener trimming overgrown trees to increase the production of higher quality fruit, microglial cells cut and eliminate fragile neurons, so the brain can produce and store higher quality thought. If this tidying up did not take place, the brain would quickly run out of room to process thoughts and ideas.

New neurons and connections that haven't been reinforced by continual use or those thoughts that haven't been mentally tagged as being important get trimmed and eliminated by the microglial cells. Once the housecleaning has been done, the brain is prepared to address, organize, and store the thoughts and ideas generated during REM sleep.

REM SLEEP, DREAMING, AND MEMORY CONSOLIDATION

The slower, steadier pattern of deep NREM sleep enhances communication among distant regions of the brain, allowing them to collaborate by sending and receiving experiences and information in preparation for the brain to do its work of memory consolidation.

Memory consolidation is the brain's amazing ability to identify, organize, and move important and newly acquired information from short-term to long-term memory. Part of this work involves connecting and linking old and novel information together in brand new ways, which is a great definition of creativity.

While we move between NREM sleep and REM sleep, the length of the intervals between the two shifts considerably during an eight-hour period. During the first half of the night, our brains are primarily concerned with NREM sleep, when neural harvesting and the sharing of information takes place. The second half of the night, we primarily experience REM sleep. We actively dream during REM sleep, and it is during this dreaming period that memory consolidation and other critical unconscious activities take place.

DREAMING AND CREATIVITY

Walker says that REM dreaming delivers "intelligent information processing that inspires creativity and promotes problem solving."[58]

In one research project, Walker and Robert Stickgold, his associate at Harvard Medical School, found their subjects could solve 15 to 35 percent more puzzles when emerging from REM sleep when compared with those who solved the puzzles during daytime waking hours or who were awakened from NREM sleep in the middle of the night.[59]

Many creative people have credited some of their most original work to a good night's rest. English poet Algernon Charles Swinburne "sat down early one night to write a poem. To his astonishment, no matter how he forced the issue, the poem would not come. He retired to bed in disgust. Upon waking in the morning, he wrote the *Ballad of Dreamland* without a halt."[60]

It's surprising how much clearer one's thinking becomes after a good night's rest. Author John Steinbeck said, "It is a common experience that a problem difficult at night is resolved in the morning after the committee of sleep has worked on it."

Many creative ideas have arrived, seemingly out of the blue, while someone slept:

- *Robert Louis Stevenson was intrigued with the concept of good and evil in personality and wanted to write a story around the idea, but a plot would not come. For two days he racked his brain looking for an idea. On the second night, he had a dream where he saw two or three scenes that eventually appeared in* Strange Case of Dr. Jekyll and Mr. Hyde. *Early the next morning, his wife recalls, "I was awakened by cries of horror from Louis. Thinking he had a nightmare, I awakened him. He said angrily, 'Why did you wake me? I was dreaming a fine bogey tale.' I had awakened him at the first transformation scene."*[61]
- *Rolling Stones guitarist Keith Richards regularly kept a guitar and a tape recorder by his bed to capture ideas that came to him in the night. One morning he awoke to see the tape recorder running. He hadn't recalled waking in the night, so he assumed that he had accidently*

pushed the RECORD button in his sleep. He rewound the tape and there, "in some sort of ghostly version, is [the main riff of the hit song 'Satisfaction']. It was a whole verse of it. And after that, forty minutes of me snoring. I actually dreamt the damned thing."[62]

- *Paul McCartney composed the melody for "Yesterday" based on a dream he had one night in 1964. "I woke up one morning with a tune in my head, and I thought, 'Hey, I don't know this tune–or do I?' It was like a jazz melody. I went to the piano and found the chords to it, made sure I remembered it, and then hawked it round to all my friends, asking what it was: 'Do you know this? It's a good little tune, but I couldn't have written it because I dreamt it.'"*[63]

When Nicole wakes up in the morning, she tries to stay in the theta state for five to fifteen minutes, which often allows her to experience a free flow of ideas about yesterday's events, to contemplate the activities of the forthcoming day, and to enjoy insights like Steinbeck describes. She does this by lying in bed and keeping her head clear of active thought. This time can be an extremely productive period of creative mental activity.

When you dream at night or wake in the morning with greater mental clarity and new ideas, you can thank the brain's glial cells and the REM sleep time for making it happen.

CONSIDER THIS BIG IDEA

We think we have too much to do to waste our time sleeping, but this attitude is a huge mistake. If you go to bed at midnight and get up at 6:00 AM, you lose anywhere from 60 to 90 percent of your vital REM sleep time, the time when the brain turns on its healing and problem-solving power. Make a commitment to get a full night's sleep, and teach your children to do the same. Remove the technology tools that keep you and your children up late. Your brain will thank you with sharper thinking and more creative ideas.

Because the act of dreaming is one of the primary ways the brain consolidates and organizes information, pay attention to your dreams. As you dream, your logical processes shut down and your creative centers engage. In this state, your mind creates new neural pathways and connects ideas in new ways.

Keep a notebook by your bed to capture what you dream about. Over time, patterns will emerge that can provide insights into your questions and concerns. For one week, track your dreams and see what interesting problem-solving work goes on in your brain while you sleep. In the mornings as you transition from sleeping to waking, give yourself at least ten minutes in bed to let your unhindered thoughts flow. Allow your newly-consolidated unconscious brain to share the previous night's connections with your conscious brain. Write your thoughts in your journal and look for patterns, insights, and imaginative solutions.

CHAPTER 8

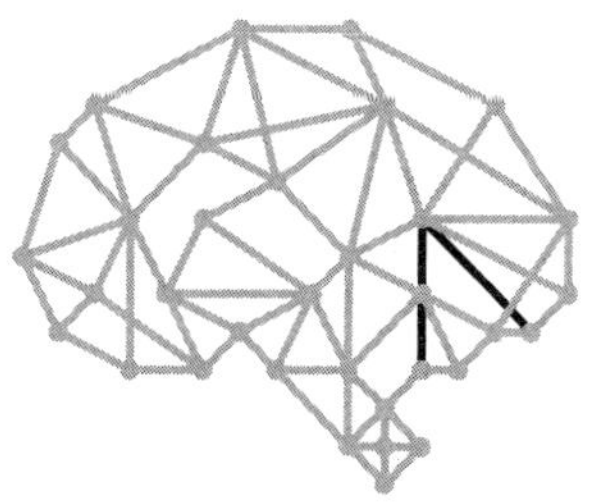

GAMMA: THE INSPIRED BRAIN

"There's so much information on the Internet. But people don't need more information, they need 'Aha! Moments,' they need awareness, they need things that actually shift and change them."
–Jack Canfield

On a fall afternoon in 1933, Hungarian physicist Leo Szilard (1898–1964) had just attended a lecture at the British Museum on the subject of the atom. The lecturer declared that although there was tremendous energy inside an atom, it couldn't be harnessed. Szilard listened to the lecture with fascination and continued to think about it after he left the museum. He was both annoyed and captivated by the presenter's dismissal of atomic energy as "moonshine."

Szilard often took random strolls around the city and let his mind wander as he walked. That afternoon as he stepped off a curb to cross the street, a world-changing thought flashed through his mind. Szilard had a vision of a small particle crashing into the heavy nucleus of an atom, like a cue ball breaking a set of billiard balls. He imagined those billiard balls crashing into other sets of billiard balls and then more and more until a giant explosion took place. The lecturer was wrong. The energy in the atom could indeed be retrieved and used. By the time he got to the other side of the street, Szilard had formulated an idea that would impact the world forever.

A few years later, a team of scientists successfully split the atom, and the Nuclear Age began. Today, entire cities are powered by the atom, an inexhaustible source of energy that came to life because of Szilard's unexpected insight in the middle of a London street in 1933.

History is full of examples of world-changing ideas that came in an instant.

For weeks, French mathematician Henri Poincare (1854-1912) had been unsuccessfully trying to prove a new mathematical theory. Disheartened and stuck, he took a break from his work and went on a trip. During this time of mental relaxation, the elusive answer arrived.

> *Just at this time I left...to go on a geologic excursion.... The changes of travel made me forget my mathematical work. Having reached Coutances, we entered an omnibus to go someplace or other. At the moment when I put my foot on the step, the idea came to me, without anything in my former thoughts seeming to have paved the way for it, that the transformations I had used to define the Fuchsian functions were identical with those of non-Euclidean geometry. I did not verify the idea; I should not have had time, as upon taking my seat in the omnibus, I went on with a conversation already commenced, but I felt a perfect*

> *certainty. On my return to Caen, for conscience sake, I verified the result at my leisure.*[64]

A few days later while working on other mathematical problems, Poincare writes of his discouragement with his lack of progress and of another similar insightful experience. "Disgusted with my failure, I went to spend a few days at the seaside and thought of something else. One morning, walking on the bluff, the idea came to me with just the same characteristics of brevity, suddenness, and immediate certainty, that the arithmetic transformations of indeterminate ternary quadratic forms were identical with those of non-Euclidean geometry."[65]

THE GAMMA SPIKE

In both Szilard's and Poincare's experiences, fully formed answers arrived in what are commonly called Aha! Moments—those sudden bursts of insight, illumination, and understanding that seemingly come out of nowhere. Had he been hooked up to an electroencephalogram machine when he stepped on the bus or as he strolled on the bluff, Poincare's dominant brainwaves would have been alpha. In both instances, his mind was at rest—always the state that immediately precedes a Big Idea or an Aha! Moment.

But the resting brain is anything but idle. Poincare's brain unconsciously but actively processed the information he had been working on in the previous weeks. In this daydreaming-like alpha state, his brain quietly and efficiently assembled, connected, and organized the information it had gathered while in beta.

Once the unconscious brain connects the appropriate information it has gathered, it shares the new connections with its conscious counterpart in a moment of illumination called a gamma spike or an Aha! Moment. Gamma spikes originate in the thalamus and sweep the brain from front to back at a rate of forty times per second, aligning and drawing different neuronal circuits to temporarily operate in complete harmony. Three-tenths of a second later, the experience transitions to the conscious brain, and in Poincare's case, he knew the solution to his problem.

Brain studies on creativity reveal what goes on in the brain when a sudden insight takes place. The brain is in alpha mode before a flash of inspiration, then high gamma wave activity comes 300 milliseconds before the Aha! Moment.[66] Neurons bind together, and disconnected brain cells link in a new neural network. Immediately after the gamma spike, the new idea enters the consciousness, as it did with Poincare as he boarded the bus. Daniel Goleman explains, "[Once the neurons] have collected more information and put it together in a novel organization... the gamma spike signals that the brain has a new insight."[67]

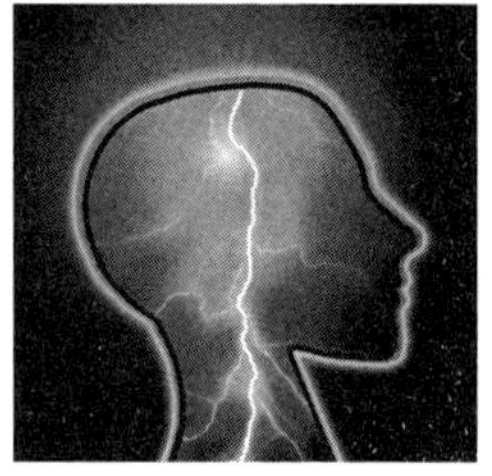

John Kounios, PhD and co-author of *The Eureka Factor: Aha! Moments, Creative Insight, and the Brain*, has done extensive study on gamma spikes. "We were amazed at the abruptness of this burst of activity—just what one would expect from a sudden insight."[68]

GAMMA BRAINWAVES

Gamma brainwaves are the fastest documented brainwave activity, and they last mere milliseconds. "There's a physical marker we sometimes feel during a gamma spike: pleasure. With the 'Aha!' comes joy. When the gamma spike hits, the heart rate rises and the brain releases 'feel good' neurotransmitters:

dopamine, serotonin, and an array of endorphins, and like Archimedes, who, as we noted, jubilantly ran naked through the streets of Greece shouting, 'Eureka, Eureka,' you have a sense of joy, completeness, and a feeling of 'rightness' that cannot be duplicated any other way."[69]

Gamma waves link and process unconnected information from all areas in the brain. People with healthy gamma wave activity tend to have better problem-solving skills, more compassion, greater self-control, higher intelligence, and keener memorization skills.

Experiments on Tibetan Buddhist monks have shown a correlation between those who regularly meditate and the production of gamma waves. A 2004 study took eight Tibetan Buddhist practitioners of meditation and monitored the patterns of electrical activity in their brains when they meditated. The researchers compared the brain activity of the monks to a group of people who meditated an hour a day for one week prior to the study.

In a normal meditative state, both groups were shown to have similar brain activity. But when the monks were asked to generate feelings of compassion during meditation, their brain activity began to fire in a rhythmic, coherent manner, suggesting gamma wave production. These gamma oscillations were the largest seen in healthy humans. Such gamma waves were almost non-existent in the novice meditators.[70]

Such research may explain the heightened sense of consciousness, bliss, and intellectual acuity people feel following meditation.

BIG IDEAS AND AHA! MOMENTS

Moments of insight that accompany gamma wave production usually prove to be very valuable. Through a series of experiments, Kounios determined that gamma spike insights often give better and more accurate solutions to problems than solutions reached by analytic thinking. "Conscious, analytic thinking can sometimes be rushed or sloppy, leading to mistakes while solving a problem. However, insight is unconscious and automatic—it can't be rushed. When the process runs to completion in its own time and all the dots are connected unconsciously, the solution pops into awareness as an Aha! Moment. This means that when a really creative, breakthrough idea is needed, it's often best to wait for the insight rather than settling for an idea that resulted from analytical thinking."[71]

Carola Salvi, PhD at Northwestern University and lead author of *Insightful Solutions Are Correct More Often Than Analytic Solutions*, writes, "The history of great discoveries is full of successful insight episodes, fostering a common belief that when people have an insightful thought, they are likely to be correct. Our study tests the hypothesis that the confidence people often have about their insights is justified."[72]

Without knowing it, Jason's coworker Nicole has discovered a thinking model that has been used by creators, thinkers, and inventors since the beginning of time. She has learned how to access wisdom, creativity, and innovative ideas by slowing her brain and allowing it to connect information in new and original ways.

It's possible for anyone to access this power, and we're going to show you how to do it.

CONSIDER THIS BIG IDEA

At a very early age, British mathematician and author Marcus Du Sautoy became addicted to the pleasant feeling that accompanied learning new things. That feeling was so wonderful, he chose to continue learning just to have it more often. Du Sautoy believes this amazing feeling is nature's way of telling us learning is a good thing, valuable for individuals and the entire human race.[73]

The feeling Du Sautoy describes is similar to the empowering feeling that accompanies an Aha! Moment or a Big Idea. It is one of the most profound emotional and intellectual experiences a person can have, often a defining moment easily recalled in detail years later that changes everything from that moment forward.

When you have an Aha! Moment, pay attention to how it makes you feel, and write it down.

You're about to unlock the secret to more Big Ideas.

PART THREE

CREATIVE THINKING MODELS

CHAPTER 9

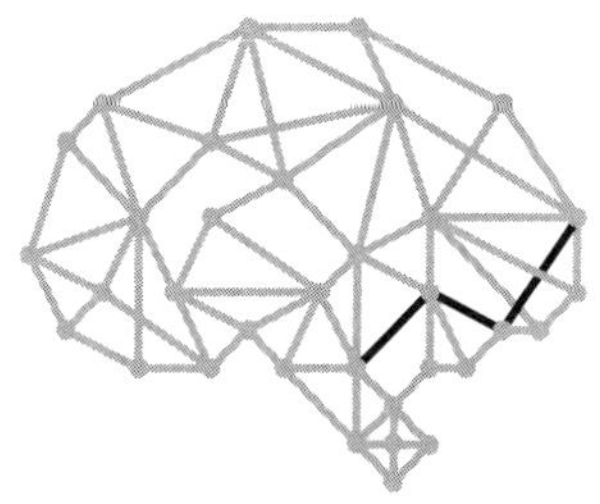

CREATIVE THINKING MODELS

"To live is to have problems, and to solve problems creatively is to grow."
–J.P. Gilford

SPEAKING TO HARVARD STUDENTS, FACEBOOK founder and CEO Mark Zuckerberg warned that the "idea of a single Eureka moment" in which a lone thinker has a groundbreaking epiphany is a myth. Zuckerberg characterized the idea of an Aha! Moment or a flash of insight as "a dangerous lie" that discourages real creativity.[74]

Zuckerberg might not believe it, but countless world-changing epiphanies *have* arrived in a single Eureka moment to some of the most brilliant women and men on the planet.

OUTSIDE IN

The ancient Greeks thought that inspired ideas were given to men and women by spirits or demons—both good and malevolent mystical beings called Muses. These ethereal, spiritual forces were believed to influence behavior and bestow thoughts and creative ideas on humans. The Muse visited, often at night, and transmitted ideas. Human minds were the vessels that captured and used those ideas.

Many people, especially creatives, still believe in the mystical Muse—an unexplainable source of inspiration that seems to float in the air—hard to harness and impossible to control.

Pulitzer Prize finalist poet Ruth Stone (1915–2011) said sometimes she could feel and hear a poem coming at her from "over the landscape." It was like a "thunderous train of air that came barreling down." When she felt it coming, "it shook the earth under her feet." Musician Tom Waits hears melodies coming from an external "genius." Johann Wolfgang von Goethe (1749–1832) claimed to have written his novella *The Sorrows of Young Werther* with hardly any conscious input, as if he was holding a pen that moved on its own.

Many world-changing discoveries have come from a single flash of insight. Einstein's theories on light, time, and gravity came in an instant, following years of mental effort. Geneticist Barbara McClintock, author J.K. Rowling, and Johannes Gutenberg all had similar experiences.

There are countless examples of people who were stuck, sometimes for years, with a problem they couldn't solve and then unexpectedly, the answer arrived fully formed. That is what happened to Archimedes when he stepped into his bath.

These sudden insights tend to come when the person has followed a centuries-old process for coming up with Big Ideas. The Aha! Moment is not a magical event for the unprepared.

CREATIVE THINKING MODELS

It is possible to gain greater access to inspiration and generate more Aha! Moments in your life. In the last hundred years, there have been a number of theories on the creative process and how to tap into the power of the brain.

THE WALLAS MODEL

In 1926, English social psychologist Graham Wallas (1858-1932) proposed one of the first models for creativity and inspired ideas. His model has four stages:

1. *Preparation–Know your field of study and be well prepared.*
2. *Incubation–Spend time away from the problem.*
3. *Illumination–Receive the "click" or "flash" of a new idea.*
4. *Verification–Determine if the "happy idea" actually solves the problem.*

THE YOUNG MODEL

In 1969, advertising executive James Webb Young (1886–1973) offered a five-step method for generating ideas.[75] It is similar to Wallas's model but includes the stage that Young calls, "working it over in your mind."

1. *The gathering of raw materials–both materials of your immediate problem and materials from a constant enrichment of your store of general knowledge*

2. *The working over of these materials in your mind*
3. *The incubating stage–where you let something besides the conscious mind do the work of synthesis*
4. *The actual birth of the idea, the "Eureka! I have it!" stage*
5. *The final shaping and development of the idea to practical usefulness*

THE ANDREASEN MODEL

Nancy C. Andreasen, psychiatrist and neuroscientist at the University of Iowa and author of *The Creative Brain: The Science of Genius*, defines creativity as "the ability to bring together disparate ideas in new and useful combinations." Andreasen has developed her own model for developing creative ideas.

1. *Preparation–an analytical time when the basic information or skills are assembled*
2. *Incubation–a more intuitive and unconscious time in which you connect the dots in a default state*
3. *Perspiration–hard work and extensive thinking about the problem*
4. *Revelation–the Eureka experience when you literally feel the tumblers of your mind click into place and you say, "A-ha, I have found the solution!"*
5. *Production–a time when insights are put into a useful form and shared with others*

THE GOLEMAN MODEL

Psychologist Daniel Goleman offers a slight variation on these models.

1. *Define the problem.*

2. *Immerse yourself in the problem.*
3. *Let it all go and let the gamma spike come to you.*
4. *Implement the solution you received during the gamma spike.*[76]

All of these models lay out similar steps to illumination, and people everywhere use variations of the models without realizing it. If you know and understand the model, you can deliberately use it to think more creatively, find better solutions to life's problems, and have more Aha! Moments.

Creative Thinking Models

Steps	Graham Wallas Model	JW Young Model	Nancy Andreasen Model	Daniel Goleman Model	Big Ideas Model The Five "I's" of Inspiration	
Step 1	Preparation	Gather information	Preparation	Define the problem	1. Identify	Write and reflect
Step 2		Digest the material		Immerse yourself in the subject	2. Ideate	
Step3	Incubation	Unconscious processing	Incubation	Let it go	3. Incubate	
Step 4	Illumination	The Aha! Moment	Perspiration Revelation	Illumination	4. Illuminate	
Step 5	Verification	Idea meets reality	Production	Implementation	5. Implement	

THE BIG IDEAS MODEL

The Big Ideas Model incorporates many of the elements proposed by earlier thinkers. The model aligns with what we know about how the mind functions, and people have been using versions of it for thousands of years. It is a summation of best practices for creative thinking. And it works!

We've assigned numbers to the steps in the Big Ideas Model, but it's important to understand that the steps do not necessarily follow each other in a rigid consecutive order. At any one time, you could be working on an aspect of each of the five steps, and they often overlap each other as you learn and practice the principles of our model.

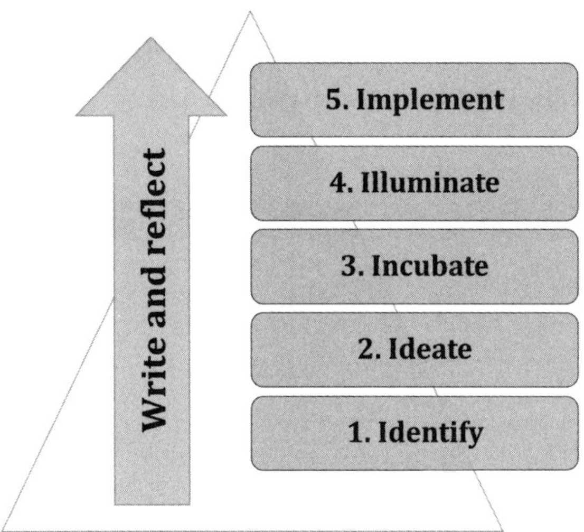

THE FIVE I'S OF INSPIRATION

- **First—Identify:** *Clearly define what you want to understand or discover.*
- **Second—Ideate:** *Develop your idea and gather information.*
- **Third—Incubate:** *Stop thinking about the problem and give your brain a chance to rest and renew.*
- **Fourth—Illuminate:** *Wait for insights to come and write them down when they arrive.*
- **Fifth—Implement:** *Put your best ideas into action.*

EINSTEIN AND THE BIG IDEAS MODEL

This model worked for Albert Einstein on more than one occasion. Theoretical physicist Michio Kaku, tells of Einstein's struggle and the eventual Aha! Moment that changed physics forever.

> *One day around May of 1905, Einstein went to visit his good friend Michele Besso, who also worked at the patent office, and laid out the dimensions of the problem that had puzzled him for a decade. Using Besso as his favorite sounding board for ideas, Einstein presented the issue: Newtonian mechanics and Maxwell's equations, the two pillars of physics, were incompatible. One or the other was wrong. Whichever theory proved to be correct, the final resolution would require a vast reorganization of all of physics. He went over and over the paradox of racing a light beam. Einstein would later recall, "The germ of the special relativity theory was already present in the paradox." They talked for hours, discussing every aspect of the problem, including Newton's concept of absolute space and time, which seemed to violate Maxwell's constancy of the speed of light. Eventually, totally exhausted, Einstein announced that he was defeated and would give up the entire quest. It was no use; he had failed.*
>
> *When he returned home that night...he remembered riding in a street car in Bern and looking back at the famous clock tower that dominated the city. He then imagined what would happen if his street car raced away from the clock tower at the speed of light. He quickly realized that the clock would appear stopped, since light could not catch up to the street car, but his own clock in the streetcar would beat normally.*
>
> *Then it suddenly hit him, the key to the entire problem. Einstein recalled, "A storm broke loose in my mind." The answer was simple and elegant: time can beat at different rates throughout the universe, depending on how fast you moved.... This meant that events that were simultaneous in one frame were not necessarily simultaneous in another frame,*

> *as Newton thought. He had finally tapped into "God's thoughts," he would recall excitedly. "The solution came to me suddenly with the thought that our concepts and laws of space and time can only claim validity insofar as they stand in a clear relation to our experiences.... By a revision of the concept of simultaneity into a more malleable form, I thus arrived at the theory of relativity."*
>
> *The day after this revelation, Einstein went back to Besso's home, and without even saying hello, he blurted out, "Thank you. I've completely solved the problem." He would proudly recall, "An analysis of the concept of time was my solution. Time cannot be absolutely defined, and there is an inseparable relation between time and signal velocity."*
>
> *For the next six weeks, he furiously worked out every mathematical detail of his brilliant insight, leading to a paper that is arguably one of the most important scientific papers of all time. According to his son, he then went straight to bed for two weeks after giving the paper to Mileva [his wife] to check for any mathematical errors. The final paper, "On the Electrodynamics of Moving Bodies," was scribbled on thirty-one handwritten pages, but it changed world history.*[77]

Can you identify the five stages of the inspired thinking process in Einstein's experience? After ten long years of deliberation, his brain finally connected the dots and delivered the foundational principles of special relativity to his consciousness in an instant. Einstein's Aha! Moment changed the world.

The rest of this book will talk in detail about the five I's of the Big Ideas Model and how you can put them into action.

Are you ready to be changed?

CHAPTER 10

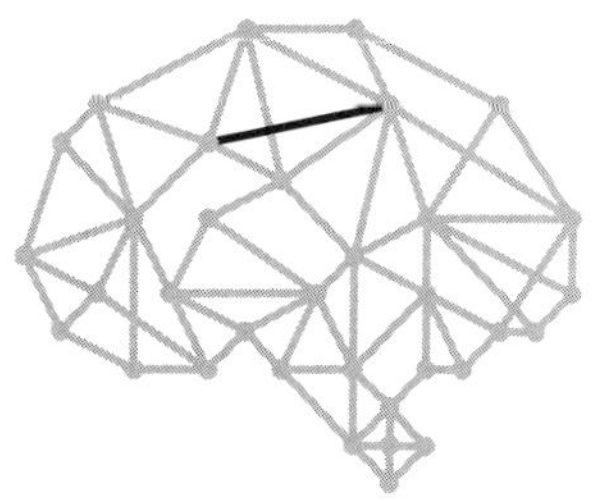

IDENTIFY

IDENTIFY · IDEATE · INCUBATE · ILLUMINATE · IMPLEMENT

"The most common source of management mistakes is not the failure to find the right answers. It is the failure to ask the right questions.... Nothing is more dangerous in business than the right answer to the wrong question."
–Peter Drucker

IN 2005, DEBBIE STERLING GRADUATED from Stanford with a degree in engineering and product design but had no idea what to do with her education. Steve Jobs spoke at Sterling's graduation, encouraging the graduates to never rest until they found their passion. Jobs' speech had a great impact on Sterling, and finding her passion became her quest. Over the next few years, she worked several different jobs and did volunteer work in India, but she didn't find the passion for her work. She kept searching.

Sterling "read every book I could get my hands on about branding, design, and marketing. I was always the last person at the office every night, putting in the extra effort on every project that came my way."[78]

Sterling started a club called "Idea Brunch," where she and some friends met once a month to discuss their latest ideas. A friend who had studied engineering with Sterling in college shared her dismay at the lack of women in their engineering classes. She had played with her brother's construction toys when she was young, and those toys had inspired her early interest in engineering. She wondered if similar toys couldn't be targeted specifically to girls.

With that idea, Sterling had her Eureka moment. "I knew instantly that it was my true passion...what I had been searching for ever since Steve Jobs' speech." GoldieBlox was born.[79]

GoldieBlox is an award-winning company that creates products to "empower girls to build their confidence, dreams, and ultimately, their futures." GoldieBlox was the first start-up with both a Super Bowl commercial and a float in the Macy's Thanksgiving Day Parade. Since its founding in 2012, GoldieBlox had over one million app downloads and has sold over one million construction toys in more than 6,000 major retailers worldwide. Sterling's passion turned out to be a Big Idea.

The first stage in the Big Ideas Model is Identify. Identifying means to clearly define what outcome you desire, what problem you need to solve, or what question you want to answer. For Sterling, her penetrating need to find work she was passionate about drove her focus and kept her moving. For Einstein, it was having a deeper understanding of the nature of light and time. For Archimedes, it was determining if a crown was pure gold.

American inventor Charles Kettering (1876–1958) holder of 186 U.S. patents, once said, "A problem well stated is a problem half solved."[80]

We think in terms of questions and answers. Questions and the ideas that follow often form the basis of our thoughts. **Learning to formulate questions and writing about those questions is the first step of the Big Ideas Model.**

If you want to have more Aha! Moments, ask questions.

THE BRAIN'S FILTERING SYSTEM

One day in 1948, a supermarket executive visited Drexel Institute of Technology in Philadelphia with a request. He needed a simple way to track his inventory to make pricing easier for his employees and checkout easier for his customers. Bernard Silver, a physics professor at the Institute, overheard the conversation and asked graduate student Joseph Woodland to help him find a solution. Woodland got so absorbed in the problem, he quit his graduate student teaching position and moved in with his grandfather so he could spend more time working on it. But a solution did not easily come.

Mentally exhausted after working on the problem for weeks, Woodland went to the seashore to relax. While sitting on the beach, he ran his fingers through the sand, making dot and dash marks like the Morse code he had learned as a Boy Scout. Suddenly and unexpectedly, the answer to the problem came to him. Merchandise information could be encoded using lines to represent different numbers.

Although it took over twenty-five years, Woodland's Aha! Moment on the beach became the ubiquitous UPC barcode that is on virtually every item sold in stores today.

In June 1974 at a supermarket in Ohio, a packet of Wrigley's chewing gum bearing the new barcode was the first object to pass through a checkout scanner. The packet is now on display at the National Museum of American History.

Woodland received the National Medal of Technology from President George H.W. Bush in 1992 and was eventually inducted into the National Inventors Hall of Fame together with his late colleague, Bernard Silver. In October 2013, Drexel Institute of Technology was recognized as the "The Birthplace of the Barcode."

The unconscious brain actively and continuously looks for answers to our questions.

But how does it work?

THE RAS

Harvard psychologist Jeffrey Statinover and neurophysiologist Joe Dispenza believe the brain receives an incomprehensible 400 billion bits of information per second. As large as this number is, an incredibly small percentage of this raw data—only 2,000 bits per second—makes it to the conscious brain.[81]

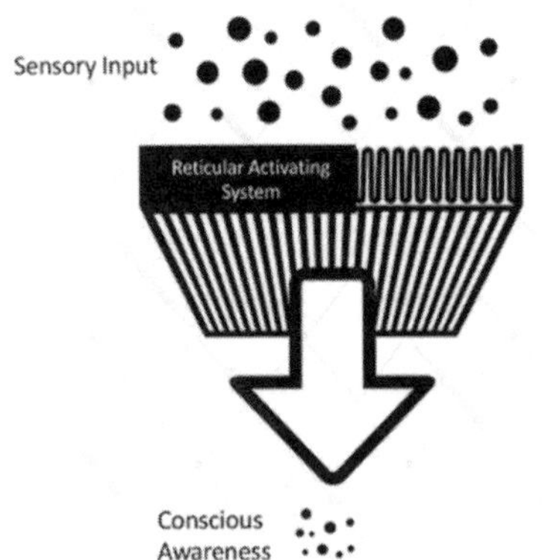

Two interrelated parts of the brain, the thalamus and a group of interconnected neuronal circuits called the Reticular Activating System or the RAS, act as the brain's input switchboard. The thalamus and the RAS discard much of the sensory information and forward the rest to different areas of the brain.

The RAS is an area of tightly packed nerve fibers and cells containing nearly 70 percent of your brain's estimated 200 billion nerve cells, 140 billion cells in total.[82]

The RAS functions as the brain's reducing valve, sometimes called an "attention filter." Without this incredible information-sifting system, we would be overwhelmed by sensory input from the outside world.

This filtering process is known as "sensory gating." Sensations from only one set of sense organs are allowed to pass at a time, while information from other senses is temporarily held back. In ways not yet fully understood, the brain prioritizes sensory input then signals the body's sense receptors, telling them to hold all calls until the brain can get around to handling them, which is why a person who is highly stimulated (i.e. in a fight or playing a sport) might not immediately feel the pain when she has been hurt.

An example of the RAS in action is a new mother who lives next to a busy airport. Despite the constant roar of airplanes over the house, the mother always hears her baby in the next room even if he makes the smallest noise. She is tuned in to her baby's voice, and the RAS filters out the airport racket. The RAS takes instructions from her conscious mind ("I need to hear my baby.") and passes it on to her unconscious mind, which becomes diligent and alert to her request.

The RAS pushes relevant and pertinent information to the conscious mind. If you buy a Volvo, you suddenly start seeing other Volvos on the road. The Volvos have always been there, but you didn't notice them before.

Your agent asks you to write Amish fiction. You didn't even know the genre existed. You start doing research and suddenly you notice Amish books at Walmart and Amish specials on TV. Amish books were there before, but they were filtered out of your consciousness by the RAS. Now the RAS lets the information through.

This experience of enhanced observation and awareness is known as the "Baader-Meinhof phenomenon."[83] You're not crazy. It's just a manifestation of the RAS doing its job.

"Your automatic creative mechanism...operates in terms of goals and end results. Once you give it a definite goal to achieve, you can depend upon its automatic guidance system to take you to that goal much better than 'you' ever could by conscious thought. You supply the goal by thinking in terms of end results. Your automatic mechanism then supplies the means."[84]

When we ask questions, the RAS goes to work to find answers.

ARE YOU CURIOUS?

Before you can ask a question, you have to wonder why.

Questions often come as a result of penetrating curiosity—the state of being intensely interested in something. A curious person doesn't need to be motivated or managed or incentivized. Curiosity, the desire to understand something at a deeper level, always precedes the question.

We start out in this world with a great deal of curiosity, but unfortunately, as we grow up, much of our innate inquisitiveness goes away. "Almost all children in their natural state ask lots of questions," says creativity author Michael Gelb. "That's how they learn so much in the first five years of life. But then we send them to school, where they learn that answers are more important than questions."[85] By the time kids are in third grade, most stop asking questions, and learning stalls. Asking questions is essential for inspired ideas to formulate. Great thinkers never stop asking questions because they know asking questions is one of the most powerful ways to learn.

Curiosity can be rekindled and nurtured. As we renew our ability to ask questions, we harness the power of curiosity to gain deeper insights and develop fresh ideas.

It all starts with wanting to know more.

Harvard biologist E.O Wilson has devoted his life to the study of ants. When asked why, he replied, "Because they're so abundant, they're easy to find, and they're so interesting."[86]

Walt Disney once said, "When you're curious, you find lots of things to do."

Thomas Jefferson sent Lewis and Clark on their exploring expedition, in part, because he was curious about what was out there "in the West." Jefferson believed Lewis and Clark might find woolly mammoths, giant sloths, and other prehistoric creatures along the upper Missouri.[87]

Curiosity expert Todd Kashdan says, "One of the best ways to better appreciate the power of curiosity is to start exercising it more consciously in your daily experiences. By doing so, you can transform routine tasks, enlivening them with new energy. You will also likely begin to notice more situations that have the potential to engage you, giving your curiosity even more opportunities to flourish."[88]

Curiosity drives questions, and questions drive inspired ideas, which is why Google gives its workforce twenty percent of their time to explore their own projects. 3M and W.L. Gore have similar programs. These companies know that the root of innovation is the unconstrained curiosity of their employees.

By its very nature, life is a springboard for questions. Some are simple, with ready-made solutions as accessible as a Google search. Other questions require answers that are not as straightforward. Existential questions about reason, meaning, and purpose are richly complex and painfully elusive. Life-transforming, world-changing questions drive explorers, philosophers, artists, and scientists. We call these questions "high stakes" questions because the hard-fought answers have the potential to change a life or the world.

FRAMING YOUR QUESTIONS

For hundreds of years, Middle Eastern nomads moved from location to location in search of water. The high stakes question was always, "Where can we find water?" Survival depended on water. When they discovered a well of water, some put down roots and stayed put. Their high stakes question became, "How can we protect our water?" Wars were waged over water. If they lost the battle or the well dried up, they moved on in search of more water.

By about 300 BC, the Romans wearied of unpredictable droughts, and instead of asking, "Where can we find water?" reframed the question. "How can we make the water come to us?" This fundamentally different question delivered a revolutionary answer. The Romans became master builders of water aqueducts. By the third century AD, the city of Rome enjoyed fresh water delivered by eleven aqueducts with a combined length of 500 miles, sustaining a population of over a million people.

The nomads and the Romans were plagued with the same water problem. The way they framed their questions to address the problem brought completely different answers. These answers shaped their civilizations for centuries. Rome's progress, ingenuity, and quality of life went unmatched for almost two millennia.

E.E. Cummings penned, "Always the beautiful answer, who asks a more beautiful question."

HOW CAN WE ASK BETTER QUESTIONS?

Questions tend to come from two directions.

First, you have a problem: There's friction in a relationship, you're deeply in debt, you or someone you love has an addiction. The company isn't making enough money to cover expenses. Sales are down. Your marketing presentation is mediocre. Your son got an F on his report card. You're tired, depressed, burned out. You can't afford to get the car fixed. Your daughter got cut from the team.

There are as many different kinds of problems as there are people in the world.

Second, you wonder why something is the way it is: Why doesn't the moon fall to the earth like an apple? What would it be like to ride a light beam? Why is their family so happy? What if I never had to worry about money again? Can I write a book? Why do uranium compounds fog photographic plates, even in the dark?

PROGRAMMING THE RAS

How do we get our unconscious brains, including the RAS, to find answers to our problems?

THERE ARE AS MANY DIFFERENT KINDS OF PROBLEMS AS THERE ARE PEOPLE IN THE WORLD.

One of the best ways to get the RAS working on a problem is by writing. The incredible benefits of writing are explored more fully in the next chapter, but it's important to know that writing is an effective way to alert the RAS regarding what's important and what should be ignored. Things take priority in the RAS once they are written down.

In *Write it Down, Make it Happen*, Henriette Anne Klauser says, "Writing triggers the RAS, which in turn sends a signal to the cerebral cortex: 'Wake up! Pay attention! Don't miss this detail!' Once you write down a goal, your brain will be working overtime to see you get it, and will alert you to the signs and signals that were there all along."[89]

A recent study of 267 people by Dr. Gail Matthews, a psychology professor at the Dominican University of California, discovered that the very act of writing down a goal increases the likelihood of its happening by 42 percent.[90] The more detail you can provide the RAS, the better.

Since the RAS filters relevant information to the conscious brain, writing down your questions increases the likelihood you'll get answers. As Tony Robbins says, "Where your attention goes, the energy flows."[91] The more you daydream about your problems, goals, and questions and the desired outcomes you want, the more likely it is you'll find answers. Clearly identifying your questions by writing about them signals the RAS that they are important to you. The RAS will get to work.

On his personal development blog, Ruben Gonzalez says, "The RAS is like Google. There are millions of web sites out there, but you filter out the ones you are not interested in simply by typing a keyword."[92] Writing down your questions and articulating your problems and the desired outcomes are the best ways we know to type keywords into the RAS.

In our inspiration workshops, we ask people to write down a few questions they would like to explore in both their professional and personal lives. Next, they choose one of the questions to consider more deeply and then write about it. We are amazed how seriously people take this assignment. Most find the writing exercise to be both liberating and enlightening, and many get unexpected, high-quality answers as they write. These are answers that might never have arrived had they not written the question down and not explored the answer through writing.

The next time you want a better solution, take some time to get clear on the problem or the question. Don't look for answers until you fully understand the question. Write your question down, and then write about your question. Getting the question right will often require writing and rewriting. The experience may take a few minutes or several hours, but the insights you receive will be profound. **Learning how to frame and define your questions is foundational to inspired thinking.**

CONSIDER THIS BIG IDEA

Make a list of ten questions you want to explore from both your professional and personal life. Choose one question and spend twenty minutes writing about it.

How do you feel? What did you learn?

To help you ask better questions:

- *Accept there is more than one way to do almost anything and there are multiple solutions to many problems.*
- *Study your surroundings with fresh eyes, as if you are seeing and doing things for the first time.*

- *Don't hold so fast to your opinions that you are unwilling to change your mind, even in the face of convincing contrary evidence.*
- *Remain open to new ideas, particularly if they are different from your own.*
- *Try to see the world from someone else's viewpoint, especially someone whose opinion might be in opposition to yours.*
- *Choose a topic you're interested in and do some research. Write an essay or a blog about it.*
- *Watch a new* TED *Talk each week.*

CHAPTER 11

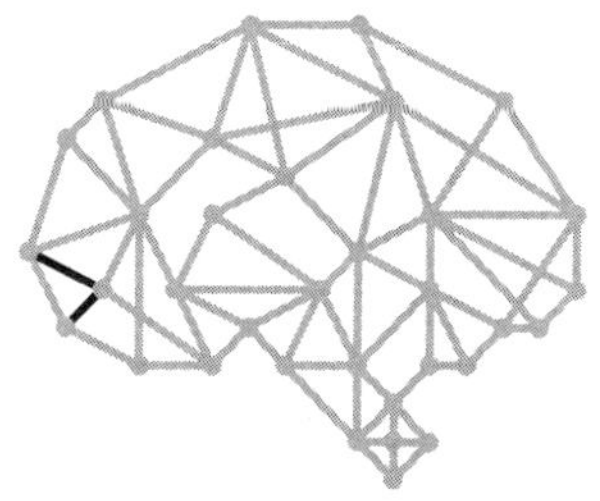

IDEATE

IDENTIFY · **IDEATE** · INCUBATE · ILLUMINATE · IMPLEMENT

"Ask, and it shall be given you; seek, and ye shall find; knock, and it shall be opened unto you: For every one that asketh receiveth; and he that seeketh findeth; and to him that knocketh it shall be opened."
–Matthew 7:7-8 KJV

IN 1752, ENGLISH PHYSICIAN WILLIAM STUKELEY (1687–1765) wrote the story of Sir Isaac Newton's (1643–1727) legendary falling apple as told to him by Newton himself. "As he sat in contemplative mood occasioned by the fall of an apple, he thought he to himself, Why should that apple always descend perpendicularly to the ground?"[93]

Newton was in a "contemplative mood," most likely an alpha state, when he sat under that tree and saw the apple fall. It is probable he was not actively thinking about apples or gravity but relaxing and letting his mind wander. The serendipitous event caused him to ask the question that became the focal point of his life's work and many of his later discoveries.

It is rarely mentioned that it took Newton twenty-two years of reflection and painstaking mental effort before he published his theory in his masterwork, *Philosophiæ Naturalis Principia Mathematica*, in 1687. What was Newton doing during those

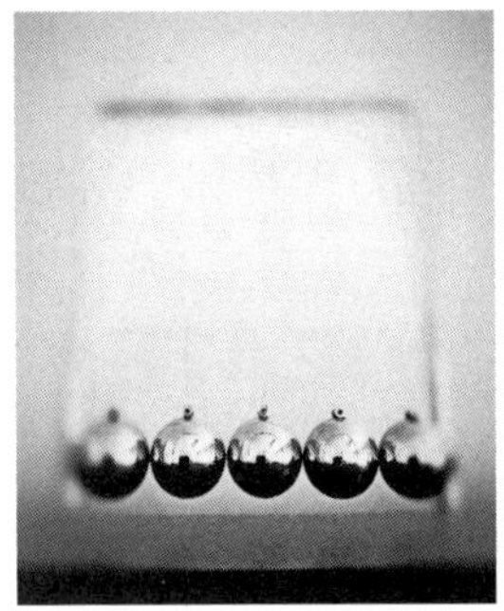

twenty-two years? He was thinking, gathering information, and writing down his ideas. He filled many vellum notebooks with his thoughts, sketches, and commentary. His surviving correspondence and manuscripts contain an estimated ten million words, enough to make up roughly 150 novel-length books.[94]

When asked how he made his discoveries, Newton responded, "By always thinking unto them. I keep the subject constantly before me and wait till the first dawnings open little by little into the full light."[95]

Although biographers have long celebrated Newton's intellect—he also pioneered calculus—it's clear his achievements aren't solely a byproduct of his stunning intelligence. Newton persistently gathered all the information he could on a certain subject and then studied and pondered his questions until he got answers, regardless of how long it took.

For years, Charles Darwin (1809-1882) actively explored the questions of natural selection and sought out every available book related to the theme of human evolution. "When I see the list of books of all kinds which I read...I am surprised at my industry."[96] Not only did Darwin study and read, he captured his thoughts in the hundreds of notebooks and journals he kept during his life.

Ben Franklin (1706–1790) a wildly productive innovator, made many of his useful contributions primarily because he was inquisitive and wrote about his questions and ideas. From a very early age, he taught himself to think deeply by asking provocative questions and by writing about the natural world and human foibles in his almanacs and newspapers.

The same tenacity can work for you. Once you've identified a question or problem, start paying attention and gathering information. You'll be astonished at the amount of relevant information just waiting to be found. Information will come from many unexpected places. Be sure to collect it, make notes about it, maybe create a file. You'll come across newspaper articles you previously ignored, seemingly written just for you. Radio stations will report stories that align with your research. Facebook posts from people you barely know will specifically address your problem. It will feel like the Universe has lined up to provide the assistance you need. Don't worry about organizing this information. Get the information into your brain and let the unconscious mind go to work.

Botanist and inventor George Washington Carver (1864–1943) was so highly regarded for his ingenuity that *Time Magazine* called him a "Black Leonardo."[97] By his own count, he devised 199 products from the peanut, 118 products from the sweet potato, 85 from the pecan, and more than 35 from the soybean.

Carver's creative methods teach us a great deal about information gathering. His most common source of new ideas was observing how people on the street or in the home used peanuts and the other crops he studied. The everyday ingenuity of common people was often the inspiration for his more refined and sophisticated innovations. Carver made no secret of his methods. "Inspiration is never at variance with information," he wrote. "In fact, the more information one has, the greater will be the inspiration."[98] Carver understood information drives inspiration, and information can come from most anywhere.

PAYING ATTENTION

If you pay attention to the information coming your direction, the RAS will pay attention too. If you disregard relevant data, over time, the RAS will filter it out and stop pushing it to your conscious brain. "What good is eternity when most can't manage a half an hour well?" Ralph Waldo Emerson once said. The same can be said about inspiration. What good are world-changing ideas when we can't manage the slightest inspired thought?

Sometimes inspiration is subtle. It enters the mind when the brain has slowed down, like when you're in the shower or driving to work or watching children play at the park. It generally comes as a fleeting thought, and if you don't capture it, the important idea might be lost forever.

Paying attention, especially to something as wispy as a thought or a feeling, takes work. Mindfulness, the exercise of cultivating focused, nonjudgmental awareness of the present moment, requires a great deal of practice.

Alison Bonds Shapiro says, "Attention is noticing and being with something without trying to change it. Attention takes the time to fully explore, to discover whatever there is to know about something, to watch as things change by themselves without our trying to 'fix' anything. Attention is patient, and attention is kind. No rush. No burden. No criticism."[99]

For many of us, our default state tends to be ignoring what's around us rather than absorbing it. According to Thorin Klosowski,

> *Being observant means watching people, situations, and events, then thinking critically about what you see. We miss a lot in the world while we're busy shuffling between here and there. While there's no way to quantify how that affects our well-being, it's clear the more you pay attention, the more often you'll come up with new ideas.*[100]

As Rick Hanson wrote in his book *Buddha's Brain: The Practical Neuroscience of Happiness, Love, and Wisdom*, "Attention shapes the brain. What we pay attention to is literally what we will build in our brain tissue. Our neurons wire in response to what we focus upon."

WRITING

American poet and Pulitzer Prize finalist Ruth Stone (1915-2011) grew up in rural Virginia. Poems would come to her as she worked the fields.

> *[Stone] would be out working in the fields, and she would feel and hear a poem coming at her from over the landscape. It was like a thunderous train of air, and it would come barreling down at her over the landscape. And when she felt it coming...cause it would shake the earth under her feet, she knew she had only one thing to do at that point. That was to, in her words, 'run like hell' to the house as she would be chased by this poem. The whole deal was that she had to get to a piece of paper fast enough so that when it thundered through her, she could collect*

> *it and grab it on the page. Other times she wouldn't be fast enough, so she would be running and running, and she wouldn't get to the house, and the poem would barrel through her and she would miss it, and it would 'continue on across the landscape looking for another poet.'*[101]

Whether it is imprints in clay, scratches on pots, or scrawls on papyrus, since the days of the Sumerians in 8,000 BC,[102] people have been writing to capture thought, transmit information, and tell stories. We have access to the minds of great thinkers like Moses, Aristotle, Galileo, Descartes, Suor Maria Celeste, Caroline Herschel, Benjamin Franklin, Margaret Mead, and Thomas Jefferson primarily because they, or someone else, captured their ideas in written form.

For millennia, humans have used writing to collect and communicate ideas, to make records, to reflect on experiences, and to learn from those experiences.

Writing is a powerful tool for changing abstract ideas into intelligent constructions. Writing builds a framework of connected ideas and helps us define and refine our thoughts to gain understanding. The two activities of writing and thinking build on each other. To paraphrase novelist E.M. Forster, we write in part to know what we think.

CAPTURING IDEAS

The notion of capturing inspired ideas by writing them down has been around since humans have had the ability to draw. Some paintings on cave walls and ceilings in Europe and Indonesia are believed to be over 35,000 years old.[103]

The human brain is better at creating than remembering. This is why we make grocery lists and jot down tasks in our planners. As good as we are at keeping a list of what we need to buy for the party, most of us are less inclined to capture our random thoughts and ideas. How many good ideas have been lost simply because they weren't written down?

COMMONPLACE BOOKS

Throughout Europe in later medieval times, particularly during the Enlightenment Era, journals known as "commonplace books" were used to capture and store ideas. The commonplace book was a leather-bound journal filled with blank pages where thoughts, ideas, proverbs, quotations, speeches, and conversations could be recorded. Commonplace books were a sure sign of distinction. Every literate gentleman and many women carried one. Such books continued to be used well into modern times. A generation ago, the commonplace book was replaced by the day planner and today, by the smart phone.

Many of history's greatest thinkers like Julian of Norwich, Galileo, Hypatia, Aristotle, Plato, Teresa of Avila, Shakespeare, and Kepler were dedicated writers. They are remembered in part, because they wrote their ideas down. Over 30,000 pages of Da Vinci's personal notes were found in his home after his death. Thomas Edison filled 3,000 notebooks of 280 pages each documenting his experiments and ideas.

THE LOST ART OF WRITING

In a recent workshop, we discussed the idea of writing as a method for developing insights and getting more Aha! Moments. A twenty-two-year-old in the class rejected the idea of carrying a journal wherever he went. He said the idea simply wouldn't

WRITING ABOUT AN IDEA, PEN TO PAPER, ACTUALLY CREATES NEURAL CONNECTIONS THAT LEAD TO BIG IDEAS.

work for most people his age. Holding up his phone, he said he could text anything more quickly than writing it out. We agreed with him regarding speed. Watching how quickly and effortlessly most people navigate their phones, we know his observation is accurate.

But speed is not the goal when trying to capture and develop complex thoughts and ideas. Writing about an idea, pen to paper, actually creates neural connections that lead to Big Ideas. The creative part of the brain does its best work when it slows down, which is one of the reasons handwriting is vital to creativity and innovation.

Advancements in technology tie us closer together than ever before, revolutionizing what it means to communicate. We call our loved ones from thousands of miles away. We use FaceTime and Skype. We text and email each other at the push of a button. While these advancements have undoubtedly improved our lives, they also greatly inhibit our ability to think and create.

We need to think on a deeper level than in a text laced with emojis, acronyms, and abbreviations. As handy as it is, the smart phone has its limits as a tool for elevated thinking.

HANDWRITING VS. TYPING

Research indicates that handwriting is vastly more beneficial to learning and innovative thinking than typing or keyboarding. Handwriting slows down the brain, and when you're in alpha mode, you accelerate cerebral connections and increase the likelihood of inspired ideas.

Research by Virginia Berninger, a professor at the University of Washington, shows that writing in cursive activates massive regions in the brain involved in thinking, language, and working memory, the systems for temporarily storing and managing information. Keyboarding only activates a single region of the brain.[104]

Recent research on college courses shows that taking notes by hand is better than taking notes on a laptop, particularly for capturing and remembering conceptual information. The very act of using a pen or pencil helps you better retain information. People capture and recall up to 30 percent more information when they've taken handwritten notes rather than typed ones.[105]

Handwriting requires more effort than keyboarding, and the mental effort helps the brain make critical connections. The more effort you put into understanding something, the stronger signal you're giving your brain of its importance, which enhances the inspiration process.

"When we write, a unique neural circuit is automatically activated," says psychologist Daniel M. Oppenheimer. "There is a core recognition of the gesture in the written word, a sort of recognition by mental simulation in your brain, it seems that this circuit is contributing in unique ways we didn't realize."[106] The result? Learning is easier, connections occur, and inspired ideas flow.

WRITING BENEFITS

Writing, whether on a keyboard or with a pencil, is one of the best ways to access the hidden wisdom of the unconscious. Journaling can help you address difficult problems, find peace, and achieve mental well-being. The act of writing serves as a bridge between the conscious and the unconscious minds, where information and insights can be transferred from one to the other.

People with physical injuries who write their innermost thoughts and feelings in a journal heal more quickly than those who do not.[107]

Spending just fifteen minutes a night writing down what you're thankful for could do wonders for your sleep, according to an Applied Psychology Health and Well-Being study. Study participants who wrote down a list of things they were grateful for before bed experienced longer and better sleep.[108] The New York Times reported that people who kept a gratitude journal for two months were more optimistic about life and exercised more than people who did not keep such a journal.[109]

According to a 2005 article in the *Journal of Psychiatric Treatment*, expressive writing by hand has short- and long-term benefits. Expressive writing has been linked to improved mood, higher levels of serotonin, a stronger sense of well-being, lower stress levels, and fewer symptoms of depression, as well as the physical benefits of lower blood pressure, improved lung and liver function, and decreased time spent in the hospital.[110]

Step Two in the Big Ideas Model is Ideate. To ideate means to research, read, learn, and study. Take notes. Search, contemplate, and ponder. Become an expert. Then pay attention. Write it down, and keep writing.

CONSIDER THIS BIG IDEA

Fantasy author Stewart Stafford said, "A brainwave in your stream of consciousness ripples past but once. Fail to catch it and an idea that could change your life and the world dissipates on the water's surface and is gone forever."

As you gather data, you will be surprised at how the world will support your efforts. Information and material will come to you constantly from the most unlikely places. Pay attention to your dreams, articles online and in magazines, and conversations.

Capture your ideas in written form, even if they don't seem to make sense or have any structure. The shortest pencil is better than the longest memory. Whether you're capturing your ideas in your phone or writing them in a journal, make sure you have a special place to keep track of new ideas, inspiring quotes, or Aha! Moments. You don't know when they'll arrive.

When an Aha! Moment or inspired idea comes, turn off your internal critic. Don't assess the quality of the idea until you have the time and space to study it. The more ideas you can generate, the better. Having several ideas you'll later discard is better than having no ideas at all.

Make it a habit to write each day. Separate yourself from technology, relax, and allow your mind to wander as you write. It doesn't matter if the writing is bad or your grammar and punctuation are poor. Simply write what comes to you. After a few minutes, reread what you've written. Write a sentence, phrase, or word summarizing the most important or interesting ideas you've written about. What themes emerge? What seems to have the most significance? What has potential, tension, or surprise? Repeat this back and forth process until you feel you've made some useful discoveries.

Look for insights and gamma spikes. Pay attention.

CHAPTER 12

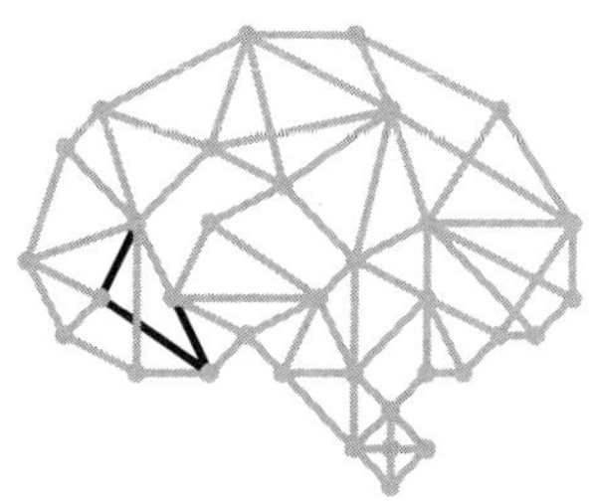

INCUBATE

IDENTIFY · IDEATE · **INCUBATE** · ILLUMINATE · IMPLEMENT

"People used to wait in line at the checkout and daydream. Now they pull out their phones and go into the digital world. This is a missed opportunity to reflect, to relax, to be mindful of the moment. Creativity lives in those quiet spaces."
–Adam Gazzely

WOLFGANG AMADEUS MOZART (1756–1791) IS regarded as one of the greatest composers in history. He composed seventeen masses, over fifty symphonies, and twenty-four operas including *The Magic Flute*, *Don Giovanni*, and *The Marriage of Figaro*. In his short life, he composed well over 600 musical works.

In the "Rochlitz Letter," the great composer described his creative process.

> *When I am, as it were, completely myself, entirely alone, and of good cheer; say traveling in a carriage or walking after a good meal or during the night when I cannot sleep; it is on such occasions that my ideas flow best and most abundantly. Whence and how they come I know not, nor can I force them. Those ideas that please me, I retain in...memory and am accustomed, as I have been told, to hum them to myself. If I continue in this way, it soon occurs to me how I may turn this or that morsel to account, so as to make a good dish of it.... All this fires my soul.*[111]

This is an apt description of the third step in the Big Ideas Model: Incubate.

To incubate means to develop slowly without outward or perceptible signs. When we let a problem or a question incubate, we stop consciously working on it and allow the brain to slow down and make new connections.

In *The River of Consciousness*, neurologist Oliver Sacks (1933–2015) emphasizes the importance of mental incubation. "Creativity involves not only years of conscious preparation and training but unconscious preparation as well. This incubation period is essential to allow the subconscious assimilation and incorporation of one's influences and sources, to reorganize and synthesize them into something of one's own."

It was only after French mathematician Henri Poincare put his work on hold and went on a geological expedition that he received his profound mathematical insight. His conscious brain was at rest, giving his unconscious brain, which likely already had the answer, the open window to his consciousness.

Productivity expert Ray Williams says, "Researchers have found that resting minds are creative minds. Numerous studies have shown that people tend to develop more novel, inventive, and innovative ideas if they allow their minds to wander....

Some companies such as Google recognized this fact and provide professional growth courses such as 'Search Inside Yourself' and 'Neural Self-Hacking' and also mindfulness meditation where the goal is to recognize and accept inner thoughts and feelings rather than avoiding or repressing them."[112]

Our best ideas don't come when we're sitting in front of a computer straining to make a project come together. It's when we get up for a break or take a walk around the block—precisely when our attention wanders away from the task at hand—that the missing piece pops into our heads. Insight almost always comes when an intensely focused mind wanders free, uninhibited by active thought.

How many times have you hit a mental block in the evening and found the answer the next morning with hardly any effort? The idea of "sleeping on it" truly does help creativity. We should never decide on a serious issue before we've had a good night's rest.

Some people have found it's easy to let their thoughts wander by wandering. Many of history's most creative thinkers and innovators used daily walks as a way to slow the brain and find new ideas.

- *Philosopher and theologian Soren Kierkegaard found his daily walks so inspiring he often hurried back to his desk and started writing, still wearing his hat and carrying his walking stick or umbrella.*
- *Inventor Nikola Tesla's idea for alternating electric currents came to him in a flash of inspiration while he was out on a leisurely stroll. So not to forget his idea, he used*

his walking stick to draw a picture in the dirt, explaining to his partner how the currents might work.[113]

- *Writer Charles Dickens religiously took three-hour, twelve mile walks every afternoon. What he observed on these strolls often found its way into his writing.*
- *Russian composer Tchaikovsky made do with a two-hour walk but wouldn't return a minute early, convinced that cheating himself of the full 120 minutes would make him ill.*
- *Beethoven took lengthy strolls after lunch, always carrying a pencil and paper with him in case inspiration struck, as it often did.*
- *Composer and pianist Erik Satie did the same on his long strolls from Paris to his working-class suburb, stopping under streetlamps to jot down notions that arose on his journey. It is rumored that when those lamps were turned off during the war years, his productivity declined as well.*[114]

Friedrich Nietzsche (1844–1900), the famous philosopher, once wrote, "All truly great thoughts are conceived while walking," a tradition that goes all the way back to ancient Greece and the Peripatetic school, literally the walking school, founded by followers of Aristotle.[115]

A recent study by Mary Oppezzo and Daniel Schwartz of Stanford University determined that creativity levels are consistently and significantly higher for those who walk for as little as five minutes before engaging in problem solving compared to those who do not.[116]

We might think it's a waste of time to interrupt work to take a short stroll, but it's actually an effective way to unleash our creativity.

Inspiration can and will come any time, even during hectic and busy days, but only if you're doing the things to invite and receive it. As we've mentioned before, the Big Ideas Model is not a rigid step-by-step process you implement in numerical order. At every step of the journey, it is important to get into alpha mode several times each day, so your brain can recharge with sodium and potassium and consolidate information.

During the summer of 1905, Austrian composer Gustav Mahler (1860–1911) hit a roadblock in his efforts to complete his seventh symphony, one he had begun the previous summer. "Two weeks long I tortured myself to distraction, as you may well remember...until I escaped to the Dolomites! There the same struggle and finally I gave up and went home in the conviction that this summer was lost to composition."

In a struggle similar to Einstein's, it seemed no matter how hard Mahler worked in beta mode, he couldn't get unstuck. It wasn't until he gave up and let his mind wander that the light finally broke through. He got into a rowboat to cross Worthersee Lake, and his mind slowed sufficiently to allow disconnected neurons to come together. "At the first dip of the oars I found my theme of the introduction to the first movement—and in four weeks the first, third, and fifth movements were done."[117]

Another example of getting to alpha and reaping the benefits of a rested brain comes from Herman Von Helmholtz (1821–1894), one of the great minds of the nineteenth century. Von Helmholtz made significant contributions to the fields of science, physiology, psychology, and philosophy.

His contributions include the principle of conservation of energy, the measurement of the speed of nerve impulses, and the invention of the ophthalmoscope used to examine the inside of the eye.

Helmholtz trained his brain by gathering information and then getting into alpha mode and letting ideas incubate:

> *Often ... [ideas] arrived suddenly, without any effort on my part, like an inspiration.... They never came to a fatigued brain. It was always necessary, first of all, that I should have turned my problem over on all sides to such an extent that I had all its angles and complexities 'in my head.' Then...there must come an hour of complete physical freshness and quiet well-being before the good ideas arrived. Often, they were there in the morning when I first awoke. But they liked especially to make their appearance while I was taking an easy walk over wooded hills in sunny weather.*[118]

In *Anatomy of Inspiration*, music historian Rosamond Harding (1899–1982) emphasized the benefits of resting your brain:

> *There is much to be said in favour of laying a work aside to mature; for one thing, it gives the judgment time to operate; the mind is able to return to the work from time to time with a fresh outlook; and check it from many different angles. It follows also that if new ideas are to be set aside to develop and newly finished works left to 'mature,' there must be several things on hand at the same time in various stages of development. The continuity of attention is purposely shorted and interrupted partly on account of the rest this gives.*[119]

CONSIDER THIS BIG IDEA

Develop the practice of "not thinking" by meditation and mindfulness. A wealth of evidence and research suggests that if you spend time in a meditative state, your brain will function more efficiently, and you'll be less anxious, more creative, and healthier.

Work on a problem by "not working on it." Define the problem, find out everything you can about it, learn and study, then let your brain rest so it can make the connections you need to receive powerful solutions.

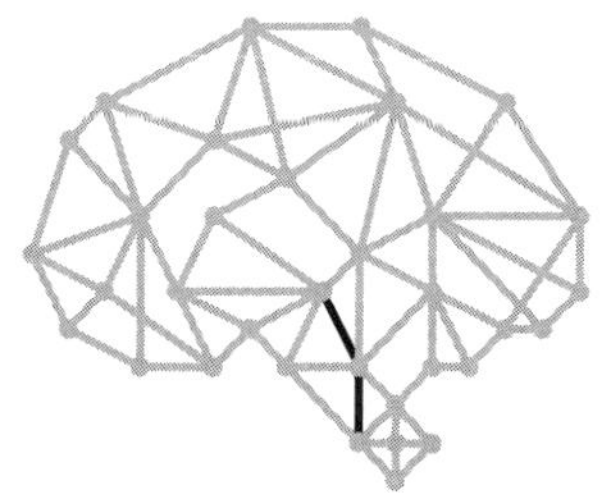

ILLUMINATE

IDENTIFY · IDEATE · INCUBATE · **ILLUMINATE** · IMPLEMENT

"Having, by a time of very intense concentration, planted the problem in my subconsciousness, it would germinate underground until, suddenly, the solution emerged with blinding clarity, so that it only remained to write down what had appeared as if in a revelation."
–Bertrand Russell

BARBARA MCCLINTOCK (1902–1992), WINNER OF THE 1983 Nobel Prize in Physiology or Medicine, is known for having had many Aha! Moments in her life.

One afternoon, McClintock stood in a cornfield with a group of scientists pondering the unexpected results of a crops genetics experiment. McClintock was so perplexed that she walked from the cornfield to her laboratory where she could sit alone and think. She spent about half an hour considering the problem when, "suddenly I jumped up and ran down to the field. At the top of the field...I shouted, 'Eureka, I have it! I have the answer! I know what this 30 percent sterility is.'"

Her colleagues insisted that she prove her sudden discovery, but she had no idea how to explain it. "It had all been done fast; the answer came, and I'd run. Now I worked it out step by step—it was an intricate series of steps— and I came out with what it was."

Decades later McClintock said, "When you suddenly see the problem, something happens that you have the answer before you are able to put it into words. It's all done subconsciously. This happened many times to me, and I know when to take it seriously. I'm so absolutely sure, I don't talk about it, I don't have to tell anyone about it, I'm just sure this is it."[120]

The fourth step in the Big Ideas Model is Illumination or the epiphany, the flash of insight, the mystical Aha! Moment. Illumination is that sudden moment of realization, recognition, and comprehension you didn't have before—the goal of the creative process.

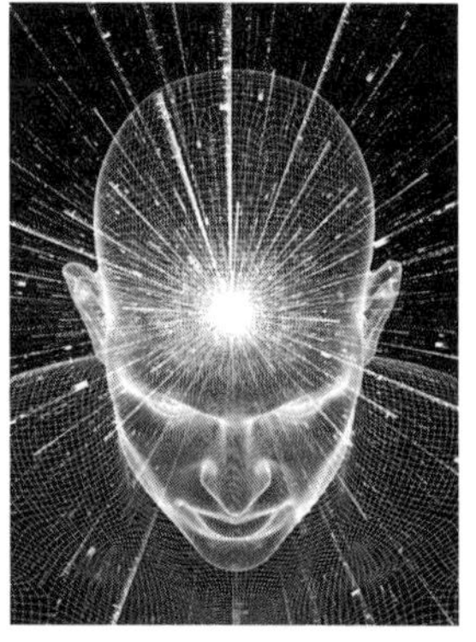

As profound as the Aha! Moment is, it is the product of the creative process rather than the starting point. It comes as a result of conscious effort and sometimes years of hard mental work. Thomas Edison said, "Genius is one percent inspiration and 99 percent perspiration."

McClintock spent years studying and thinking on her subject, which is one of reasons she had many Aha! Moments.

Illumination almost always follows a period of mental relaxation, when the brain's default mode network is active and engaged. It happened to McClintock as she walked through the cornfield and let her mind unwind.

For Frederic Eugene Ives (1856–1937), the inventor of the half-tone printing process, his moment of illumination came after a good night's rest. "While operating my photostereotype process in Ithaca, I studied the problem of half-tone process. I went to bed one night in a state of brain fog over the problem and the instant that I woke in the morning saw before me...the completely worked-out process and equipment.[121] This process, now known as the "Ive's Process," remained the standard process for photographically illustrating nearly all printed material for the next eighty years. Even today, the structure of most printed halftone images has virtually remained unchanged.

Neuroscientist Marcus Raichle confirms the process. "You accumulate all this experience and background, and then all of a sudden there's an association that your brain has rather cleverly pulled off."[122]

In 2001, Raichle was walking from his office to a nearby conference room to meet with colleagues after their paper had been rejected for publication. All of a sudden, he cracked the nut. He knew how to explain how the resting brain could be active without having been deliberately activated. He had, you might say, an Aha about Ahas. "Ten years' worth of work on activation was suddenly relevant to solving the default-mode problem."[123]

The leap would amount to the biggest breakthrough of his career. Raichle's paper on the brain's default mode has been cited more than 4,000 times. It's an affirmation of Louis Pasteur's famous quote: "Chance favors the prepared mind."[124]

SOMETIMES GAMMA SPIKES ARE GAMMA BUMPS

Not all insights come as life-changing revelations or bright flashes of light. An insight might be weighty but subtle. Sometimes the unconscious brain will give you the answer as you wander in the park, but other times the idea will come in the shower or when you're driving. The important thing is to pay attention to the insights you have, both large and small. Some are gamma spikes. Others are profound but more indirect. Still others are small but meaningful and helpful in your day-to-day life.

Several years ago, Craig put one of his teenage sons into a drug rehab program. The program required him and his wife to spend two to three hours, two nights a week at the facility. It also required them to take four of the other students in the program to their home to eat and sleep every night and to have them back to the facility by eight o'clock the next morning.

At the same time, another one of their sons was in a cardiac intensive care unit awaiting a heart transplant. After four major surgeries, his defective heart had finally worn out. Their son's health deteriorated every day and his life hung in the balance. It was a stressful time for the whole family.

One night, during this unusually difficult period, Craig had a life-changing dream. In the dream, he was in a college psychology class. The professor in the dream had just returned a multiple question essay test. Craig's corrected test was plastered with red pen marks. Craig was overwhelmed and wondered how he had done so poorly on the test. The professor put his arm around Craig, looked him in the eye, and said, "You will get this, but you have to pay attention." Craig woke with a start and wrote down the dream. To what did the professor want him to pay attention?

NOT ALL INSIGHTS COME AS LIFE-CHANGING REVELATIONS OR BRIGHT FLASHES OF LIGHT. AN INSIGHT MIGHT BE WEIGHTY BUT SUBTLE.

This wise professor, who Craig has now come to believe was his unconscious mind, was reminding Craig to learn as much as he could from his life's experiences.

It's one thing to have hard experiences and quite another to learn from them. All learning takes effort. When we don't pay attention and neglect to write things down, much of the wisdom we might have gained from hard experience is lost. To go through a difficult life experience without learning something is the ultimate waste. If we make the effort to learn from our experiences, we grow and change for the better.

CONSIDER THIS BIG IDEA

How to have more moments of illumination:

1. *Go on regular walks and let your mind wander.*[125] *Take a notebook to capture ideas when they arrive.*
2. *Make meditation a habit. As little as ten minutes twice a day will bring tremendous benefits. Meditate at least ten minutes before working on projects that require creative thought. You'll come up with more and better ideas as a result.*[126]
3. *Think happy thoughts. Happy people are prone to get more and better ideas than unhappy or anxious people. Smile. Based on studies by James Laird, even forced smiling tricks the brain into thinking you are happy, and you actually become happier.*[127]
4. *Listen to cheerful music. Happy music improves cognition and enhances learning. Researcher Gene Rowe discovered that people who listen to happy music are far more creative than people who do not.*[128]

5. *Try to get eight hours of sleep every night so you get plenty of* REM *sleep, which is where creative thought is heightened.*[129]
6. *Pay attention to your hunches. Hunches are pre-Aha! Moments.*
7. *Capture your insights in a notebook, a journal, or on your phone. Don't let those Big Ideas go to waste.*

CHAPTER 14

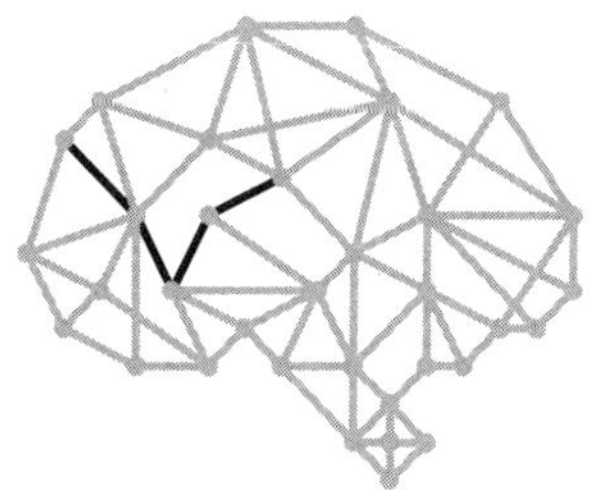

IMPLEMENT

IDENTIFY · IDEATE · INCUBATE · ILLUMINATE · **IMPLEMENT**

"For an Aha! Moment to transform the world, it isn't enough for someone to experience it; the person who experienced it must subsequently do something with that moment."
–William B. Irvine

IN THE TWENTY YEARS SINCE the first Harry Potter novel was published, J.K. Rowling's Harry Potter brand has grown to be worth more than twenty-five billion dollars. The books have collectively sold more than 500 million copies, making them the bestselling book series of all time, with the final four novels repeatedly setting records for the fastest selling books in history. The series has been translated into seventy-three languages and adapted into eight incredibly popular films, as well as inspiring spin-off books, films, and a lucrative body of related merchandise.[130] *The Wizarding World of Harry Potter* is one of the most popular attractions at Universal Studios Florida. *Harry Potter and the Cursed Child* won six Tony awards on Broadway, including Best Play.

The idea of Harry Potter was born while Rowling sat on a train after an exhausting weekend looking for an apartment. "I was travelling back to London...on a crowded train, and the idea for Harry Potter simply fell into my head," Rowling says. "I had been writing almost continuously since the age of six, but I had never been so excited about an idea before. To my immense frustration, I didn't have a pen that worked, and I was too shy to ask anybody if I could borrow one...so I simply sat and thought for four hours, while all the details bubbled up in my brain, and this scrawny, black-haired, bespectacled boy who didn't know he was a wizard became more and more real to me."[131]

Rowling wrote down her ideas that very evening, but her circumstances delayed the book's completion for over three years. It was four more years before *Harry Potter and the Philosopher's Stone* was finally published. During that time, Rowling's mother passed away of complications from multiple sclerosis, and following a failed romance, Rowling relocated from England to Portugal and back again. When she moved to Edinburgh, Scotland with her newborn daughter, Rowling found herself in dire straits, a situation she would later describe as "poor as it is possible to be in modern Britain without being homeless." But acting on the inspiration she had received on the train years earlier, Rowling had the grit to chip away at the book.

But what if she had given up on her Big Idea?

KAMAL MEATTLE

Air pollution in New Delhi, India kills thousands of people annually. Those with asthma are hit especially hard. Kamal Meattle, the owner of a software development company, was slowly dying with every breath he took. He knew he had to do something to save his health but had no idea where to start.

One day while walking through the city's botanical gardens, he had an Aha! Moment. "Plants produce oxygen and consume toxins! I could fill my office building with oxygen-producing plants!"

But the insight couldn't improve his health or change his life until he actually implemented it.

Meattle found a way to make his building relatively airtight then filled his offices with three different kinds of plants that generate abundant oxygen, clean pollutants from the air, and do so without needing a lot of sunlight. "With enough of those plants, a person could literally be in a bottle with a cap on top and they would need no other source of fresh air."

Meattle no longer suffers from debilitating asthma, and his employees have fewer allergies and headaches. Their eyes no longer burn at work, and they take fewer sick days. What Meattle didn't expect was a twenty percent increase in measurable productivity and a fifteen percent decrease in his power bills. [132]

AMIGOS OF HONDURAS

When Dave Riley was nineteen, he served as a missionary in Honduras, where he got a sense of how difficult life is for most of the people who live there. When he came back to the United States, his question was, "How can I help the people of Honduras?" This question percolated in his brain for over thirty years.

One evening as Dave and his wife, Leona, watched the news, a strong impression came that they needed to do something for the people of Honduras, but neither of them knew anyone in the country and had no idea what they should do. The following day, Dave called a friend who had also spent time in Honduras. They decided to act on Dave and Leona's Big Idea and go to Honduras to see how they could help.

Amigos of Honduras, a nonprofit humanitarian organization, was born. Amigos of Honduras builds schools, arranges microloans, assists in the planting of saleable crops, provides food and Christmas gifts for thousands of children, and oversees clean water projects in over thirty Honduran villages.

That is a Big Idea put into action!

IMPLEMENTATION

One of the biggest challenges after an Aha! Moment is following through on the idea in spite of the inevitable difficulties that arise.

J.K. Rowling, Kamal Meattle, and Dave and Leona Riley acted on inspiration. **Implementation is the final step in the Big Ideas Model.** Implementation requires the most determination and courage of all the steps because no matter how inspired an idea is, it takes an unusual amount of tenacity, perseverance, and unyielding vision to turn it into a reality.

Johannes Gutenberg's revolutionary idea came to him "as a ray of light." It took Gutenberg over ten years after his experience to find the money and build the prototypes, ten years to take his brilliant idea from concept to reality. Had he not been so tenacious, the idea might have died. What if he had decided it was just too hard and given up?

Remember how thrilled Archimedes was when he discovered the principle of displacement? He ran through the streets naked shouting, "I have found it!" The day after his revelation on the nature of light, Einstein rushed into his friend's house exclaimed, "I have completely solved the problem!" In her autobiography, Helen Keller shared the feeling she had the moment she understood that objects had names. She says the idea, "Awakened my soul, gave it light, hope, joy, set it free!"

Perhaps the main reason inspiration feels so good is because innovative ideas blaze new trails for us on a personal level as well as on a grander scale. Whether it's moving to a new city, starting a new company, or writing a book, Big Ideas take desire, focused determination, and emotional toughness. Some people will do their very best to talk you out of taking risks, exploring the unknown, or trying new things. If inspiration weren't accompanied with a feeling of "rightness," most of these important ideas would likely get tossed aside.

What if after three thousand attempts to find the filament,[133] Edison had given up on the light bulb? It was his remarkable vision of what could be and what should be that kept him going.

Doing something that's never been done before is risky. The chances of failure are high. But your inspired idea will shrivel and die if you don't act.

MAKE A BIG IDEA ACTION PLAN

A Big Idea will remain just that, a big idea, unless you do something with it after it comes. When you have a Big Idea, it's time to develop an action plan. Consider writing about the following questions:

- *Why am I energized by this Big Idea?*
- *What specific steps do I need to take to make this Big Idea happen?*
- *Who can help me?*
- *How exactly could people support me in this?*
- *What skills do I need to turn this Big Idea into reality?*
- *Whom do I know who has done something like this before?*
- *What resources and tools might be worth acquiring?*
- *What are the risks involved in making my Big Idea happen?*
- *What might get in the way?*
- *What else might be required to help me bring this Big Idea to life?*
- *How much will it cost?*
- *What is my timeline?*

The purpose of developing a plan is to gain clarity as to what might be required to bring your Big Idea to fruition. Greater clarity drives confidence and understanding, which will help you to take the necessary steps to make your Big Idea happen.

CONSIDER THIS BIG IDEA

Your Aha! Moment only has the power to change the world if you act on it. Decide if your idea has value then make a plan, set goals, and take action.

Weighty, world-changing ideas aren't the only ones you should pay attention to. In reality, you won't get many, if any, of those in your lifetime. But personal, life-changing ideas can and will come as you follow the Big Ideas Model. You might get insights into ways to mend a relationship, grow a company, tell a story, paint a picture, teach a child, write a song, or improve your health.

You have the power to change your life and maybe change the world. But only if you act.

CHAPTER 15

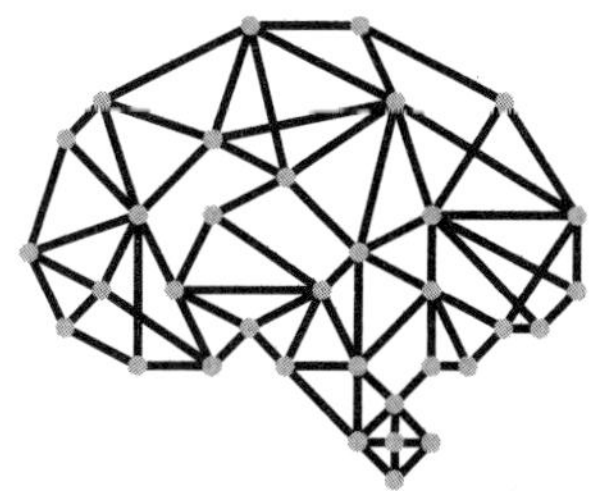

FINAL THOUGHTS

YOU'RE HOLDING IN YOUR HAND one of the most powerful tools for innovative thinking you will ever read—a way to harness the power of your brain to get more Aha! Moments, Eureka experiences, and Big Ideas.

The Big Ideas steps are straightforward and intuitive:

1. **Identify** *the problem.*
2. **Ideate** *by gathering information.*
3. **Incubate** *and let it go.*
4. **Illuminate** *by paying attention and capturing the Big Ideas when they come.*
5. **Implement** *your new idea by taking action.*

Keep track of the process by writing about it. We can't overemphasize the importance of writing things down. Writing slows the brain, signals the RAS to pay attention, and helps the brain link unconnected ideas. Writing will help you identify the right questions, organize your thoughts, and gain clarity. Writing ignites the creative mind.

Armed with this knowledge, you're ready to take on the world. You're ready to write that book, paint that picture, compose that symphony. You can balance your company's budget, nail that presentation, or increase your sales numbers. You'll be able to mend that broken relationship, strengthen your family, and improve your health.

Greater wisdom, better answers, and groundbreaking insights are just a few steps away. You've learned how to generate life-transforming, possibly world-changing, ideas. You know what you need to do and how to do it.

Having immersed ourselves in the Big Ideas principles for years, we understand how life-changing they can be. We also understand how difficult it is to actually make these changes. Be patient with yourself. We all want great ideas, and we tend to want them right now. It's hard to wait for a truly inspired idea, but the wait is a crucial part of this incredible process.

Aha! Moments and Big Ideas don't come easily. Accessing new ideas requires serious thinking, and elevated thinking takes work. Remind yourself what is at stake: a new idea, a better way to do something, a precious relationship, or an amazing discovery. You can change your life. You can change the world.

You have problems—mind-bending, frustrating, annoying problems.

You need solutions. You need good ideas, and you need to know how to get them. And not just good ideas, but profound, focused, life-changing ideas.

Big Ideas.

You've just found the way.

Go get 'em!

BIG IDEAS TRAINING

LIKE THE BOOK? GET THE TRAINING and take your personal and business creativity to a whole new level.

Take a deeper dive and learn how your work team or group can apply the Big Ideas concepts by scheduling a Big Ideas workshop. Help your people think more imaginatively and innovatively, regardless of their areas of focus. In today's world, creativity is needed in virtually every profession and arena.

Big Ideas Training is for individuals, groups, businesses, and organizations that want better ideas and cutting-edge, innovative solutions and for anyone desiring a competitive edge.

Big Ideas Training is one of the most interesting and useful workshops you'll ever attend.

For more information call **801-891-3277** or go to **www.bigideastraining.com**.

Find *Big Ideas* on Facebook at: **Big Ideas: Unleash Your Creative Self**

BIG IDEAS KEYNOTE SPEECH

Would you like to share these gripping ideas with your group or organization? Have Craig Case, Jennifer Beckstrand, or another Big Ideas presenter share these time-proven, often ignored concepts in an impactful and highly relevant keynote speech at your next function or gathering.

These presentations are entertaining, engaging, and inspiring, full of valuable insights for anyone looking for better solutions in their professional or personal lives.

For more information call **801-891-3277** or go to **www.bigideastraining.com**.

BIG IDEAS PODCAST

Get added ideas on ways to advance your thinking with the Big Ideas podcast, featuring some of the most innovative and interesting ideas on brain theory and creativity.

Find it at: **www.bigideastraining.com/podcast**.

ENDNOTES

INTRODUCTION

[1] Burke, James. *The Day The Universe Changed*, Little Brown and Co., 1987, p. 303.

[2] Andrews, Evan. https://www.history.com/news/history-lists/11-innovations-that-changed-history, Dec 18, 2012.

[3] https://www-03.ibm.com/press/us/en/pressrelease/31670.wss, May 18, 2010.

CHAPTER 1 – THE NATURE OF BIG IDEAS

[4] Perse was the pseudonym of Marie Rene Auguste Alexis Leger, who won the Nobel Prize for Literature in 1960.

[5] Isaacson, Walter. *Einstein: His Life and Universe*, 2007 Simon & Schuster, p. 549, See also *Literature and the Metaphoric Universe in the Mind* by Nicolae Babuts, Taylor & Francis, 2017.

[6] Thrash, Todd; Elliot, Andrew J. *Inspiration as a Psychological Construct*, http://www.psych.rochester.edu/research/apav/publications/documents/2003_ThrashElliot_Inspirationasapsychologicalconstruct.pdf: evocation, transcendence, and approach motivation, 2003.

[7] Ibid.

[8] http://paidtoexist.com/inspiration-vs-motivation/#99.

[9] Lepore, Meredith. https://www.levo.com/posts/aha-moments-to-inspire-you-levo100, Sept 22, 2015.

CHAPTER 2 – STUCK

[10] Puccio, Gerard. *The Creative Thinkers Tool Kit*, The Teaching Company. LLC, www.thegreatcourses.com, 2014.

[11] Michalko, Michael. http://creativethinking.net/a-simple-way-to-get-ideas/#sthash.Rh1xxDeb.dpbs, Oct 6, 2014.

[12] Murray, Liz. *Breaking Night: A Memoir of Forgiveness, Survival, and My Journey from Homeless to Harvard*, Hachette Books, 2010, p. 246.

[13] Popova, Maria. *Elizabeth Gilbert on Inspiration, What Tom Waits Taught Her About Creativity, and the Most Dangerous Myth for Artists to Believe*, https://www.brainpickings.org/2015/06/12/elizabeth-gilbert-nypl/.

[14] McFall, Patrick. *Brainy young James wasn't so daft after all, The Sunday Post*. Apr 23, 2006.

CHAPTER 3 – THREE MINDS

[15] *Einstein the Greatest*, http://news.bbc.co.uk/2/hi/science/nature/541840.stm, BBC, Nov 29, 1999.

[16] Eagleman, David. *Incognito: The Secret Lives of the Brain*, Knopf Doubleday Publishing Group, 2012, p. 8.

[17] Gladwell, Malcolm. *Blink: The Power of Thinking Without Thinking*, Back Bay Books, 2005, p. 8–11.

[18] Tryon, Warren W. https://www.sciencedirect.com/topics/neuroscience/unconscious-mind, 2014.

[19] Tryon, W. W. *Cognitive neuroscience and psychotherapy: Network Principles for a Unified Theory*. New York: Academic Press, 2014, p. 397–451.

[20] Aquinas, *Summa theologiae*. https://dhspriory.org/thomas/summa/FP/FP087.html#FPQ87OUTP1, Benziger Bros. Edition, Translated by the Fathers of the English Dominican Province, 1947, no page numbering.

[21] Leibniz, Gottfried W. *New Essays on Human Understanding*, Chapter V – Sensation and Experience, 1765.

[22] *Freud's Model of the Human Mind*, Journal Psyche, http://journalpsyche.org/understanding-the-human-mind/.

[23] Kahneman, Daniel. *Attention and Effort*, https://pdfs.semanticscholar.org/eeb9/7f210404ca6758c6cfe41cbe552feed5f59e.pdf, 1973.

[24] Cloosterman, Annemieke. *Unconscious Mind*, https://www.mindstructures.com/unconscious-mind/.

[25] McLeod, S. A. *Unconscious mind*, www.simplypsychology.org/unconscious-mind.html, 2015.

[26] Irvine, William. *A Toast to Your Unconscious Mind*, https://blog.oup.com/2015/02/toast-unconscious-mind/, Feb 13, 2015.

CHAPTER 4 – BRAINWAVES

[27] Epstein, Robert. *The Empty Brain*, https://aeon.co/essays/your-brain-does-not-process-information-and-it-is-not-a-computer.

[28] Eagleman, David. *Incognito: The Secret Life of the Brain*, Pantheon Pub., 2011, p. 1.

[29] https://www.thenakedscientists.com/forum/index.php?topic=51418.0, May 17, 2005.

CHAPTER 5 – BETA: THE WORKING BRAIN

[30] Ling, Jacqueline. *The Physics Factbook, An Encyclopedia of Scientific Essays*, https://hypertextbook.com/facts/2001/JacquelineLing.shtml.

[31] Schilling, David Russell. *Knowledge Doubling Every Twelve Months, Soon to be Every 12 Hours*, http://www.industrytap.com/knowledge-doubling-every-12-months-soon-to-be-every-12-hours/3950, Apr 19, 2013.

[32] Schaffhauser, Dian. *College Students More Distracted Than Ever*, https://campustechnology.com/articles/2016/01/20/research-college-students-more-distracted-than-ever.aspx, Jan 20, 2016.

[33] Carr, Nicholas. *The Shallows: What the Internet is Doing to Our Brains*, W.W. Norton and Co. p. 122.

[34] *All Things Considered*, http://www.npr.org/templates/story/story.php?storyId=127370598, Jun 2, 2010.

[35] Arce, Nichole. *Texting is more dangerous than drugs, alcohol while driving: study*, http://www.techtimes.com/articles/8185/20140609/texting-is-more-dangerous-than-drugs-alcohol-while-driving-study.htm.

[36] https://productivitytheory.com/multitasking-lower-iq/, Jun 9, 2014.

[37] Matthews, Donna. *Turn Off That Smartphone, Mom and Dad!*, https://www.psychologytoday.com/us/blog/going-beyond-intelligence/201711/turn-smartphone-mom-and-dad, Nov 23, 2017.

[38] https://www.hcp.med.harvard.edu/ncs/.

[39] Denizet-Lewis, Benoit. *Why Are More American Teenagers Than Ever Suffering From Severe Anxiety?*, https://www.nytimes.com/2017/10/11/magazine/why-are-more-american-teenagers-than-ever-suffering-from-severe-anxiety.html, Oct 11, 2017.

[40] Twenge, Jean M. *Have Smartphones Destroyed A Generation?*, https://www.theatlantic.com/magazine/archive/2017/09/has-the-smartphone-destroyed-a-generation/534198/, Sept, 2017.

[41] *Does TV Make You Smarter?*, http://tvsmarter.com/documents/brainwaves.html.

[42] Neal, Megan. *Is Watching TV Actually A Good Way to Rest Your Brain?*, https://motherboard.vice.com/en_us/article/3daqaj/is-watching-tv-actually-a-good-way-to-rest-your-brain, Jan 18, 2016.

[43] Thorson, Esther; Lang, Annie. *The Effects of Television Videographics and Lecture Familiarity on Adult Cardiac Orienting Responses and Memory*, http://journals.sagepub.com/doi/abs/10.1177/009365092019003003, Jun 1, 1992.

[44] Cahn B.R.; Polich, J. (2006). *Meditation states and traits: EEG, ERP, and neuroimaging studies. Psychological Bulletin.* 132 (2): 180–211. PMID 16536641. doi:10.1037/0033-2909.132.2.180; Chiesa A.; Serretti, A. A *systematic review of neurobiological and clinical features of mindfulness meditations,* Psychological Medicine. 40 (8): 1239, 1252. PMID 19941676. doi:10.1017/S0033291709991747, 2010.

[45] See Megan Neal, *Is Watching TV Actually A Good Way to Rest Your Brain?*

CHAPTER 6 – ALPHA: THE RENEWING BRAIN

[46] https://www.transparentcorp.com/research/HuangPsychologicalEffectsBrainwaveEntrainmentPDF.php.

[47] Forrest, Michael, D. *The sodium-potassium pump is an information processing element in brain computation,* https://www.ncbi.nlm.nih.gov/pmc/articles/PMC4274886/, Dec 23, 2014.

[48] http://www.band4lifellc.com/what-are-alpha-waves/.

[49] Diaz, Alicia Lynn. soulofhealingsummit.com.s3.amazonaws.com/transcripts/Niraj_Naik.pdf, 2016.

[50] Amishi, Jha P.; Krompinger, Jason; Michael J. Baime. *Mindfulness training modifies subsystems of attention,* https://link.springer.com/article/10.3758/CABN.7.2.109#page-1, Jun, 2007.

[51] *Stress, Meditation, and Alzheimer's Disease Prevention: Where The Evidence Stands,* https://www.ncbi.nlm.nih.gov/pubmed/26445019, 2015.

[52] Gard, T.; Holzel, B.K.; Lazar, S.W., *The potential effects of meditation on age-related cognitive decline: a systematic review.* https://www.ncbi.nlm.nih.gov/pubmed/24571182, Jan, 2014.

[53] Zeidan, F.; Martucci, K.T.; Kraft, R.A.; Gordon, N.S.; McHaffe, J.G.; Coghill, R.C., *Brain Mechanisms Supporting Modulation of Pain by Mindfulness Meditation,* https://www.ncbi.nlm.nih.gov/pmc/articles/PMC3090218/, Oct 6, 2011.

[54] Smith, Fran. *How Science is Unlocking the Secrets of Addiction,* http://www.nationalgeographic.com/magazine/2017/09/the-addicted-brain/, September 2017.

[55] Popova, Maria. *The Dalai Lama's Daily Routine and Information Diet.* https://www.brainpickings.org/2015/06/09/pico-iyer-the-open-road-dalai-lama/.

[56] http://highexistence.com/arianna-huffington-interview/.

CHAPTER 7 – THETA & DELTA: THE CREATIVE BRAIN

[57] Walker, Matthew. *Why We Sleep: Unlocking the Power of Sleep and Dreams,* Scribner. Kindle Edition, p. 45.

[58] Ibid, p. 219.

[59] Ibid, p. 224.

[60] Harding, Rosamond. *An Anatomy of Inspiration*, Frank Cass & Co., Jan 1, 1967, p. 32.

[61] Balfour, Graham. *The Life of Robert Louis Stevenson*. II. New York: Charles Scribner's Sons, 1912, p. 15–16.

[62] Fox, James. *The Life of Keith Richards*, Little, Brown and Co., 2010, p. 176.

[63] Lennon, J., McCartney, P., Harrison, G.; Starr, R., *The Beatles Anthology*, San Francisco, CA: Chronicle Books, 2000, p. 175.

[64] Popova, Maria. *Inclining the Mind Toward "Sudden Illumination:" French Polymath Henri Poincare on How Creativity Works*, https://www.brainpickings.org/2013/08/15/henri-poincare-on-how-creativity-works/.

CHAPTER 8 – GAMMA: THE INSPIRED BRAIN

[65] http://www.is.wayne.edu/drbowen/crtvyw99/poincare.

[66] Goleman, Daniel. *Emotional Intelligence Blog*, http://www.danielgoleman.info/maximize-your-aha-moment/, Mar 20, 2013.

[67] Ibid.

[68] Kounios, John; Beeman, Mark. *The Eureka Factor: Aha Moments, Creative Insight, and the Brain*, Random House Publishing Group, Kindle Edition, 2015, Kindle Locations 1089–1090.

[69] Migliore, Lauren. *The Aha! Moment: The Science Behind Creative Insight*, http://brainworldmagazine.com/the-aha-moment/, May 13, 2018.

[70] Lutz A.; Greischar L.L.; Rawlings N.B.; Ricard M.; Davidson R.J, *Long-term meditators self-induce high amplitude gamma synchrony during mental practice*, Proceedings of the National Academy of Sciences USA. 101:16369–16373. Nov 16, 2004.

[71] See Kounios and Beeman, Mark. *The Eureka Factor: Aha Moments, Creative Insight, and the Brain*, Kindle Locations 1089-1090.

[72] Salvi, Carola; Bricolo, Emanuela; Kounios, John; Bowden, Edward; Beeman, Mark. *Insight solutions are correct more often than analytic solutions*, https://www.ncbi.nlm.nih.gov/pmc/articles/PMC5035115/, Feb 5, 2016.

[73] Du Sautoy, Marcus. *The Great Unknown: Seven Journeys to the Frontiers of Science*, Penguin Books, 2017.

CHAPTER 9 – CREATIVE THINKING MODELS

[74] Zuckerberg, Mark. *Mark Zuckerberg's Commencement Address at Harvard*, https://news.harvard.edu/gazette/story/2017/05/mark-zuckerbergs-speech-as-written-for-harvards-class-of-2017/, May 25, 2017.

[75] Young, James Webb. *A Technique for Producing Ideas*, Amazon Digital Services, 2015.

[76] Goleman, Daniel. *Emotional Intelligence Blog*, http://www.danielgoleman.info/maximize-your-aha-moment/, Mar 20, 2013.

[77] Kaku, Michio. *Einstein's Cosmos: How Albert Einstein's Vision Transformed Our Understanding of Space and Time*, Weidenfeld & Nicolson, 2010, p. 60–63.

CHAPTER 10 - IDENTIFY

[78] Gross, Elana Lyn. *How The Founder Of GoldieBlox Is Creating The Next Generation Of Women In STEM*, https://www.forbes.com/sites/elanagross/2017/10/11/how-the-founder-of-goldieblox-is-creating-the-next-generation-of-women-in-stem, Oct. 11, 2017.

[79] Ibid.

[80] Levy, Mark. *A Problem Well-stated is Half-solved*, http://www.levyinnovation.com/a-problem-well-stated-is-half-solved/.

[81] https://cienciaemnovotempo.wordpress.com/categorias/fisica-neurociencia/how-much-information-processing-the-brain/.

[82] Ness, Elaine. *The Reticular Activating System–Your Brain's Screening Device*, http://graciousliving.typepad.com/the_write_event/2007/08/the-reticular-a.html, Aug 28, 2007.

[83] Kershner, Kate. *What's the Baader-Meinhof phenomenon?*, https://science.howstuffworks.com/life/inside-the-mind/human-brain/baader-meinhof-phenomenon.htm.

[84] Maltz, Maxwell. *Psycho-Cybernetics*, TarcherPerigee Pub. 2016, p. 41.

[85] DesMarais, Christina. *7 Things Leonardo da Vinci Can Teach You About Creativity*, https://www.inc.com/christina-desmarais/7-things-leonardo-da-vinci-can-teach-you-about-creativity.html, Aug 6, 2013.

[86] Irvine, William B. *Aha: The Moments of Insight That Shape Our World*, Oxford Press, p. 150.

[87] Jewett, Thomas. *Jefferson and the West*, https://www.varsitytutors.com/earlyamerica/jefferson-primer/jefferson-west.

[88] Kashdan, Todd. *The Power of Curiosity*, https://experiencelife.com/article/the-power-of-curiosity/, May, 2010.

[89] Pinola, Melanie. *Why You Learn More Effectively By Writing than Typing*, http://lifehacker.com/5738093/why-you-learn-more-effectively-by-writing-than-typing, Jan 21, 2011.

[90] https://www.dominican.edu/academics/lae/undergraduate-programs/psych/faculty/assets-gail-matthews/researchsummary2.pdf.

[91] https://www.tonyrobbins.com/career-business/where-focus-goes-energy-flows/.

CHAPTER 11 – IDEATE

[92] Gonzalez, Ruben. http://www.ptonthenet.com/articles/The-Neuroscience-of-Success-2914, Aug 24, 2007.

[93] Stukeley, William. *Memoirs of Sir Isaac Newton's Life*, F.R.S. Edited by A. Hastings White, Taylor & Francis, Ltd., 1936, page number unknown.

[94] Mann, Adam. *The Strange, Secret History of Isaac Newton's Papers*, https://www.wired.com/2014/05/newton-papers-q-and-a/, May 14, 2014.

[95] See Stukeley, William M.D., *Memoirs of Sir Isaac Newton's Life*.

[96] https://charles-darwin.classic-literature.co.uk/the-autobiography-of-charles-darwin/ebook, p. 20.

[97] *The Black Leonardo*, Time Magazine, Nov 24, 1941.

[98] Kremer, Gary R. *George Washington Carver in His Own Words*, Columbia: 1987, University of Missouri Press: 1991.

[99] Shapiro, Alison Bonds. *Paying Attention*, https://www.psychologytoday.com/blog/healing-possibility/201007/paying-attention, Jul 11, 2010.

[100] Klosowski, Thorin. *How to Boost Your Observation Skills and Learn to Pay Attention*, https://lifehacker.com/how-to-boost-your-observation-skills-and-learn-to-pay-a-1678229721, Jan 8, 2015.

[101] Davis, Lizzie. https://incameralucida.wordpress.com/2013/02/13/on-ruth-stone-and-being-chased-by-a-poem/, Feb 13, 2013.

[102] *Omniglot–The online Encyclopedia of Writing Systems and Languages. Sumerian*, https://www.omniglot.com/writing/sumerian.htm

[103] https://en.wikipedia.org/wiki/Cave_painting

[104] Bounds, Gwendolyn. "How Handwriting Trains the Brain," *The Wall Street Journal*, Oct 5, 2010.

[105] *Take Notes by Hand for Better Long-term Comprehension*, http://www.psychologicalscience.org/index.php/news/releases/take-notes-by-hand-for-better-long-term-comprehension.html, Apr 24, 2014.

[106] Mueller, Pam A.; Oppenheimer, Daniel, M. *The Pen Is Mightier Than the Keyboard: Advantages of Longhand Over Laptop Note Taking*, https://cpb-us-w2.wpmucdn.com/sites.udel.edu/dist/6/132/files/2010/11/Psychological-Science-2014-Mueller-0956797614524581-1u0h0yu.pdf, Jan 16, 2014.

[107] Rodriguez, Tori. "Writing Can Help Injuries Heal Faster," *Scientific American*, Oct 17, 2013

[108] Chan, Amanda, L. *6 Unexpected Ways Writing Can Transform Your Health*, http://www.huffingtonpost.com/2013/11/12/writing-health-benefits-journal_n_4242456.html, Nov 12, 2013.

[109] Brody, Jane, E. *A Positive Outlook May Be Good for Your Health*, https://www.nytimes.com/2017/03/27/well/live/positive-thinking-may-improve-health-and-extend-life.html?mcubz=0, Mar 27, 2017.

[110] Baikie, Karen A.; Wilhelm, Kay. "Emotional and physical health benefits of expressive writing," *Advances in Psychiatric Treatment*, vol. 11, 2005, p. 338–346.

CHAPTER 12 – INCUBATE

[111] Einstein, Alfred. *Mozart's Handwriting And The Creative Process*, https://www.jstor.org/stable/43873168?seq=1#page_scan_tab_contents, Sept, 1939, p. 145–153.

[112] https://www.psychologytoday.com/blog/wired-success/201408/reflection-and-doing-nothing-are-critical-productivity.

[113] Kaufman, Scott Barry. *Wired to Create: Unraveling the Mysteries of the Creative Mind*, Penguin Publishing Group, 2015, p. 39.

[114] Carmichael, Sarah Green. *The Daily Routines of Geniuses*, https://hbr.org/2014/03/the-daily-routines-of-geniuses, Mar 19, 2014.

[115] Vishton, Peter M. *Outsmart Yourself Brain-Based Strategies for A Better You*, The Great Courses, Transcript, p. 232 233.

[116] Wong, May. *Stanford Study Finds Walking Improves Creativity*, https://news.stanford.edu/2014/04/24/walking-vs-sitting-042414/, Apr 24, 2014.

[117] Hewett, Ivan. *Mahler Year: Symphony No 7*, http://www.telegraph.co.uk/culture/music/classicalmusic/8126390/Mahler-Year-Symphony-No-7.html, Nov 11, 2010.

[118] McKendrick, John Gray. *Hermann Ludwig Ferdinand von Helmholtz, Masters of Medicine*, Longmans, Green & Company, 1899, p. 286–287.

[119] Harding, Rosamond E. M. *Anatomy of Inspiration*, Routledge, 1st edition, 1967, p. 25.

CHAPTER 13 – ILLUMINATE

[120] See Kounios and Beeman, *The Eureka Factor*, Kindle Location 466.

[121] Young, James Webb. *A Technique for Producing Ideas*, Amazon Digital Services, Nov 2015.

[122] Grierson, Bruce. *Eureka!* https://www.psychologytoday.com/us/articles/201503/eureka, Jun 13, 2018.

[123] Ibid.

[124] Ibid.

[125] Oppezzo, Marily. *Want To Be More Creative? Go For A Walk*, https://www.healthstatus.com/health_blog/wellness/want-to-be-more-creative-go-for-a-walk-marily-oppezzo/.

[126] Vishton, Peter M. *Outsmart Yourself: Brain-Based Strategies to a Better You, Lecture 9*, The Great Courses, 2016.

[127] Schnall, Simone; Laird, James Douglas. *Keep Smiling: Enduring Effects Of Facial Expressions And Postures On Emotional Experience*, https://www.researchgate.net/publication/279775059_Keep_smiling_Enduring_effects_of_facial_expressions_and_postures_on_emotional_experience, Sept, 2013.

[128] https://martinaf.com/tag/contemplative-neuroscience/.

[129] Cai, Denise J.; Mednick, Sarnoff A.; Harrison, Elizabeth M.; Kanady, Jennifer C.; and Mednick Sara C. *REM, not incubation, improves creativity by priming associative networks*, http://www.pnas.org/content/106/25/10130, Jan 13, 2009.

CHAPTER 14 – IMPLEMENT

[130] http://www.abc.net.au/news/2017-06-26/harry-potter-effect-how-seven-books-changed-childrens-publishing/86302.

[131] Dundar, Keelie. https://prezi.com/5xvj2fvhgaul/untitled-prezi/, Apr 30, 2013.

[132] Meattle, Kamal. *How to Grow Fresh Air,* Ted Talk Summary, https://tedsummaries.com/2014/11/08/kamal-meattle-how-to-grow-fresh-air, Nov 8, 2014.

[133] *The Edisonian,* http://edison.rutgers.edu/newsletter9.html, Volume 9, Fall, 2012.

BIBLIOGRAPHY

Ayan, Jordan. *Aha!: 10 Ways to Free Your Creative Spirit and Find Your Great Ideas*, Crown/Archetype. Kindle Edition, 2010.

Baker, Dan Cameron. *What Happy People Know: How the New Science of Happiness Can Change Your Life for the Better*, Macmillan, 2010.

Bargh, John. *Before You Know It: The Unconscious Reasons We Do What We Do*, Touchstone, 2017.

Berger, Warren. *A More Beautiful Question – The Power of Inquiry to Spark Breakthrough ideas*, New York, Bloomsbury Publishing, 2014.

Block, Stanley H.; Block, Carolyn Bryant. *Come to Your Senses*, Simon & Schuster, Inc., 2007.

Brockman, John. *The Mind: Leading Scientists Explore the Brain, Memory, Personality, and Happiness* (Best of Edge Series). HarperCollins, 2011.

Brockman, John. *Thinking - The New Science of Decision-Making, Problem-Solving and Prediction*, New York, HarperCollins, 2013.

Cabane, Olivia Fox; Pollack, Judah. *The Net and the Butterfly: The Art and Practice of Breakthrough Thinking*, Penguin Publishing Group. Kindle Edition, 2017.

Carey, Benedict. *How We Learn: The Surprising Truth About When, Where, and Why It Happens* Random House Publishing Group. Kindle Edition, 2014.

Carr, Nicholas. *The Shallows: What the Internet Is Doing to Our Brains*, Paperback, W. W. Norton & Company, 2011.

Carroll, Richard. *Mindfulness: How To Stop Worrying, Eliminate Stress & Change Your Life By Living In The Present - A Practical Guide To Awakening, Happiness, Love & Wisdom*, Kindle Edition, 2016.

Christensen, Clayton M.; Allworth, James; Dillon, Karen. *How Will You Measure Your Life?*, HarperBusiness, 2012.

Colvin, Geoff. *Talent Is Overrated: What Really Separates World-Class Performers from Everybody Else*, Penguin Group, 2008.

Duckworth, Angela. *Grit: The Power of Passion and Perseverance*, Scribner. Kindle Edition, 2016.

Duhigg, Charles. *The Power of Habit: Why We Do What We Do in Life and Business*, Random House Publishing Group. Kindle Edition, 2012.

Du Sautoy, Marcus. *The Great Unknown: Seven Journeys to the Frontiers of Science*, Penguin Books, 2017.

Dweck, Carol. *Mindset: The New Psychology of Success*, Random House, Inc. Kindle Edition, 2006.

Frankl, Viktor E. *Man's Search for Meaning*, Ailax Merchandise, 2008.

Franklin, Benjamin. *The Autobiography of Benjamin Franklin*, Public Domain Books.

Furr, Nathan; Ahlstrom, Paul. *Nail It then Scale It: The Entrepreneur's Guide to Creating and Managing Breakthrough Innovation*, NISI Publishing. Kindle Edition, 2013.

Gelb, Michael, J., *How to Think Like Leonardo da Vinci – Seven Steps to Genius Every Day*, New York City, Bantam Doubleday Dell Publishing Group, 1998.

Gladwell, Malcolm. *Blink: The Power of Thinking Without Thinking*, Back Bay Books, 2005.

Gladwell, Malcolm. *Outliers: The Story of Success*, Little Brown and Co. 2008.

Goldstein, Elisha. *The Now Effect: How a Mindful Moment Can Change the Rest of Your Life*. Atria Books. Kindle Edition, 2012.

Goleman, Daniel. *The Brain and Emotional Intelligence: New Insights*, More Than Sound LLC. Kindle Edition, 2011.

Grant, Adam. *Originals: How Non-Conformists Move the World*, Penguin Publishing Group. Kindle Edition, 2016.

Grosso, Michael. *Irreducible Mind: Toward a Psychology for the 21st Century*, Rowman & Littlefield Publishers. Kindle Edition, 2013.

Harding, Rosamond. *An Anatomy of Inspiration*, Frank Cass & Co. LTD, 2nd ed., 1967.

Heath, Chip; Heath, Dan. *Made to Stick: Why Some Ideas Survive and Others Die*, Random House, Inc., Kindle Edition, 2007.

Irvine, William B. *Aha! The Moments of Insight That Shape Our World*, Oxford University Press, 2005.

Isaacson, Walter. *Einstein – His Life and Universe*, Simon & Schuster, 2007.

Isaacson, Walter. *Leonardo da Vinci*, Simon & Schuster, Kindle Edition, 2017.

Johansson, Frans. *The Click Moment: Seizing Opportunity in an Unpredictable World*, Penguin Publishing Group, Kindle Edition, 2012.

Johnson, Steven. *Where Good Ideas Come From*, Penguin Publishing Group. Kindle Edition, 2010.

Kahneman, Daniel. *Thinking, Fast and Slow*, Farrar, Straus and Giroux. Kindle Edition, 2011.

Kaku, Michio. *The Future of the Mind: The Scientific Quest to Understand, Enhance, and Empower the Mind*, Knopf Doubleday Publishing Group, Kindle Edition, 2014.

Kaku, Michio. *Einstein's Cosmos: How Albert Einstein's Vision Transformed Our Understanding of Space and Time,* W.W. Norton and Co., Kindle Edition, 2010.

Kaufman, Scott Barry. *Wired to Create: Unraveling the Mysteries of the Creative Mind*, Penguin Publishing Group, Kindle Edition, 2015.

Kiefer, Charles F. *The Art of Insight: How to Have More Aha! Moments*, Berrett-Koehler Publishers, Kindle Edition, 2013.

Kounios, John; Beeman, Mark. *The Eureka Factor: Aha Moments, Creative Insight, and the Brain*, Random House Publishing Group, Kindle Edition, 2015.

Lanouette, William. *Genius in the Shadows: A Biography of Leo Szilard, the Man Behind the Bomb*. Skyhorse Publishing, Kindle Edition, 2013.

Lehrer, Jonah. *How We Decide*, Mariner Books; Reprint edition, Kindle Edition, 2010.

Maltz, Maxwell. *Psycho-Cybernetics*, Deluxe Edition, Tarcher Perigee, 2016.

Miller, Caroline Adams; Frisch, Michael B. *Creating Your Best Life: The Ultimate Life List Guide*, Sterling Press, 2011.

Neill, Michael. *The Inside-Out Revolution: The Only Thing You Need to Know to Change Your Life Forever*, Hay House UK Ltd., Kindle Edition, 2013.

Niemiec, Ryan M. *Mindfulness and Character Strengths*, Hogrefe Publishing, Kindle Edition, 2013.

Peterson, Christopher; Seligman, Martin E. P. *Character Strengths and Virtues: A Handbook and Classification*, Oxford University Press, 2004.

Pinker, Steven. *How the Mind Works*, W. W. Norton & Company, Kindle Edition, 2009.

Radin, Dean. *The Conscious Universe: The Scientific Truth of Psychic Phenomena*, HarperCollins, Kindle Edition, 2010.

Randall, Lisa. *Knocking on Heaven's Door: How Physics and Scientific Thinking Illuminate the Universe and the Modern World*, HarperCollins, Kindle Edition, 2011.

Rothenberg, Albert; Hausman. Carl, R. *The Creativity Question*, Duke University Press, 1976.

Rosenblum, Bruce; Kuttner, Fred. *Quantum Enigma: Physics Encounters Consciousness*, Kindle Edition, 2011.

Seligman, Martin E. P. *Flourish: A Visionary New Understanding of Happiness and Well-being*, Atria Books. Kindle Edition, 2011.

Sobel, Dava. *Longitude: The True Story of a Lone Genius Who Solved the Greatest Scientific Problem of His Time*, Kindle Edition, 2010.

Stull, Craig; Myers, Phil; Meerman, David Scott. *Tuned In: Uncover the Extraordinary Opportunities That Lead to Business Breakthroughs*, Kindle Edition, 2008.

Tegmark, Max. *Our Mathematical Universe: My Quest for the Ultimate Nature of Reality*, Knopf Doubleday Publishing Group, Kindle Edition, 2014.

Van Lommel, Pim. *Consciousness Beyond Life: The Science of the Near-Death Experience*, HarperCollins, Kindle Edition, 2010.

Wilson, Timothy D. *Strangers to Ourselves*, Harvard University Press, Kindle Edition, 2004.

Winters, Robert W. *Accidental Medical Discoveries: How Tenacity and Pure Dumb Luck Changed the World*, Skyhorse Publishing, Kindle Edition, 2016.

Young, James Webb. *A Technique for Producing Ideas*, Amazon Digital Services, Kindle Edition, 2015.

INDEX

ABOUT THE AUTHORS

CRAIG CASE

For over twenty-five years, Craig has enjoyed a fruitful career as a business consultant, executive coach, and trainer with some of the most successful companies in the world. Craig has spent his life and career studying and teaching personal productivity, creativity, and innovation. He has presented and spoken to audiences as large as ten thousand people in over 30 countries around the world.

Craig is a contributing author of the book, *The Wellness 8* by Jeremy Reynolds, *All The Right Reasons* by Kevin Guest, and co-author of *Big Ideas: How to Unleash Your Creative Self and Have More Aha! Moments* with Jennifer Beckstrand.

JENNIFER BECKSTRAND

Jennifer Beckstrand has a degree in mathematics and a background in editing and technical writing. Jennifer is the co-author of *Big Ideas: How to Unleash Your Creative Self and Have More Aha! Moments* with Craig Case and a contributor to *All the Right Reasons* by Kevin Guest.

Jennifer has been nominated for the coveted RWA RITA® Award for her romantic fiction writing. She is the author of *The Matchmakers of Huckleberry Hill* Amish romance series and *The Honeybee Sisters* series for Kensington Books. Jennifer's books have received starred reviews from *Publisher's Weekly* and Top Pick awards from *RT Book Reviews*. Jennifer has written twenty-one Amish romances.